Kerry Downes
was educated by the Benedictines and
at the Courtauld Institute. An expert on eighteenth-century architecture, he is well known as author of a number of books, including volumes on Wren and Vanbrugh as well as on Rubens and English Baroque and Georgian architecture. He is Emeritus Professor of History of Art at Reading University and a past President of the Society of Architectural Historians of Great Britain.

WORLD OF ART

Printed in Singap

1 NICHOLAS HAWKSMOOR (1661–1736), by Sir Henry Cheere

Hawksmoor

KERRY DOWNES

THAMES AND HUDSON

Reprinted 1996

ISBN 0-500-20096-3

Printed and bound in Singapore by C.S. Graphics

Contents

This book is dedicated to Nicholas Hawksmoor and to his many admirers in the present day

Preface

This preface will appear in print almost exactly a decade after my previous book on the subject, which is now out of print. Hawksmoor's reputation has risen steadily to an extent I should not have dared to predict in 1959: this process, as my Dedication is intended to acknowledge, is due to the artist, through his works, and to the response of the architectural public. In 1962 the Hawksmoor Committee, formed by a group of enthusiasts to publicize in particular the grave disrepair of two of the Stepney churches, secured the co-operation of the Arts Council of Great Britain in mounting an unprecedented and very successful exhibition of drawings, models and photographs. An artist of such striking individuality will never be a popular idol, but his public is now far more substantial, and vocal, than ever before.

Ten years ago the primary needs were to fight battles, ventilate problems and establish evidence. The present book is intended neither to summarize nor to supersede the earlier, though perhaps to supplement it in so far as research and thought have not stopped in the intervening decade. It is to be hoped that those readers who miss footnotes will be accommodated by the earlier book and the recent publications listed in the Bibliography. It is evident to me that exploring a subject twice does not exhaust it, and leaves some areas almost untouched. In the sense that rearranging my subject in a more nearly chronological grouping has exposed new links and comparisons, it is proper to talk of a reappraisal. I have, however, found no reason to change substantially my view of Hawksmoor in relation to his equally remarkable colleagues Wren and Vanbrugh.

This book owes much of its proximate impetus, and some of its composition, to the occasion of a Visiting Lectureship at Yale University in the Spring of 1968 and to the enthusiasm of graduate students and others at Yale and Princeton. I should like to acknowledge in particular the encouragement in Princeton of Robert J. Clark and Pierre du Prey, and at Yale the observations of Neil Levine and Walter Langsam on Castle Howard and Blenheim respectively. At home I am especially indebted to Margaret Whinney, who read the book in manuscript and made many valuable suggestions; also to Howard Colvin, Terry Friedman, John Harris and D. A. Johnson who have given me information or discussed problems. My thanks are also due to those owners of drawings who have again allowed them to be reproduced.

The final acknowledgment is a sad one which I am nonetheless glad to make. For many years the late Martin Howe had been collecting material for a fully documented book on Hawksmoor, and in particular the churches. After his death his executor made this material available to me through the Society of Architectural Historians of Great Britain, on the sole condition that any use made of it should be acknowledged. While many of Mr Howe's researches had duplicated mine or were beyond their scope, his work on the architect's genealogy has been of especial value to the present book. All Mr Howe's notes and transcripts are now deposited in the Library of the Royal Institute of British Architects, where they may be consulted on the same condition.

Department of Fine Art,
University of Reading.
June 1969

CHAPTER ONE

Learning

The accidents of historical survival present some artists to us almost entirely through their works; others appear to us as more clearly definable personalities about whom we know far more as people, through surviving correspondence and other documents. In the case of Nicholas Hawksmoor, a considerable body of work survives, but its identity for the modern world, as well as what we may call the architect's image, depends largely on documentary studies. We are fortunate in having over five hundred drawings either from his own hand or made under his direction: these are really part of his architectural work although they are hidden in libraries and museums. There are also about 170 letters which throw much light on his ideas and methods of working, and – less explicitly – on his personality.

Hawksmoor's career was to an unusual degree that of a back-room boy. He was first the pupil, then the valued assistant, and perhaps finally the partner of Sir Christopher Wren, and in the last year of the seventeenth century and the first years of the eighteenth he worked for, and with, Mr (later Sir) John Vanbrugh. The obituary attributed to his son-in-law would have us believe that he was not merely valuable but indispensable to these colleagues, and this opinion probably stems from Hawksmoor's own remarks, since a similar sentiment is to be found in some of his later letters. He was overshadowed in life (and in genius) by Wren, and in later history by Vanbrugh, and it is surely a fitting but also ironical conclusion to so obscurely brilliant a career as his that his last executed work should be the self-effacing completion of a great medieval monument, familiar to the world but recognized by few: the towers of Westminster Abbey.

Ills. 2, 184

The hidden genius whose work supports the figurehead is sometimes a real character but always a romantic one. Wren and Vanbrugh were ready to give credit where it was due, but from Hawksmoor's own testimony – as well as much other evidence and indeed common sense – his artistic partnerships were in no way one-sided. There are abundant contemporary references to all three men, although not so many as to tell us all the answers; oblivion came after death. When Hawksmoor, the last of the three, died in 1736 his style, which belonged with Wren's and Vanbrugh's to the peculiar English late bloom of Baroque, was out of fashion in favour of the urbane Renaissance revival which we remember as Georgian and which is associated in particular with the name of Palladio. Wren was too much a universal figure to be forgotten, and St Paul's Cathedral could not, as a national heirloom, be despised or ignored, but he lacked – by eighteenth-century standards – the supreme virtue of Taste. Vanbrugh, whose name is bound to that of Blenheim, was rehabilitated towards the end of the century by the open praise of Reynolds and Robert Adam. Hawksmoor's œuvre included no such cynosure. The auction of nearly two thousand of his drawings in 1740 seems to have drawn little attention, and from the unique extant copy of the sale catalogue it appears that most of those drawings have been lost. Lord Burlington acquired Hawksmoor's collection of drawings by John Webb for Greenwich, which are now in the Royal Institute of British Architects, and some of Hawksmoor's own drawings which were bought by the antiquary George Vertue have come down to us, but most of the extant drawings were not in the sale. Vertue also copied out the obituary notice, and we thus owe it to him that the account of the architect in Horace Walpole's *Anecdotes of painting*, based on Vertue's note-books, is fuller and more sympathetic than, for example, the account of Vanbrugh. The *Anecdotes* was the first history of British art, and quite independently of the fortune of his buildings a sympathetic thread runs through the writers who borrowed from Walpole.

2 London. Westminster Abbey Towers

Nevertheless, while Hawksmoor's learning, ingenuity, inventiveness and experience earned him the friendship, respect, encouragement and sponsorship of Wren and Vanbrugh, the highest offices eluded him to an extent that cannot be entirely accounted for even by the combination of changing fashion and political jobbery in the Royal Works (p. 141). There seems to be some parallel with John Webb almost exactly half a century earlier, who stood in the same relation to Inigo Jones as Hawksmoor did to Wren. Both were thorough professionals trained by masters who had come to architecture from another activity. The failure of these two men, exceptionally gifted and trained, to get right to the top, must be partly a matter of personality, but it is worth considering whether, in an age when there was no architectural profession as such, both men suffered as a result of that very professionalism which made them exceptional. It is possible to see in this failure also an early effect of that preference for the amateur or the mandarin, at the expense of the 'mere professional', which has by no means disappeared from the English economy. Without question they were the two best trained English architects of the seventeenth century; this is enough to distinguish them both from their great self-taught teachers and from the amateurs, gentlemen, master masons and deputy-paying office-holders who make up the architectural scene of their times.

Ill. 1 The only reasonably authentic likeness of the architect is the plaster bust, painted black to resemble bronze, in the Buttery of All Souls College, Oxford. It dates from the last years of his life, and the companion bust in the Buttery has a pedestal with the date 1736. It is in accordance with the self-effacing humility of much of his life (though not of his works) and of his wish to be buried 'in Shenley church yard in the county of Hertford or in some other church yard belonging to some other country village' that his likeness stands above the serving dishes of the college for which he made so many grand designs, facing the likeness of the college manciple. (In 1961 the College presented a bronze cast to the National Portrait Gallery.) We see him in casual, not Roman, dress, without a wig. The sculptor, who is assumed to be Henry Cheere but may be the young Roubiliac working in Cheere's studio, has contrived by the informality of dress and pose to persuade us that this is how his sitter really appeared. The turning of both head and shoulders and the sensitive modelling bring to life a disillusioned and experienced man who has fought and suffered a good deal. He is also, the sculptor suggests, something of a sage or a poet; less precisely and more accurately, a dreamer as well as a doer.

Nicholas Hawksmore, as his legal name seems to have been, or Hawksmoor as he usually wrote it, was very probably born in 1661, of a yeoman farming family, at East Drayton, a small village near the River Trent in the north-east corner of Nottinghamshire. His family home is identifiable from his will; the numerous but not complete records of Hawksmoors living

3 Bath Abbey. Hawksmoor's sketch, 1683

at East Drayton and neighbouring villages make it reasonably certain that his father, also Nicholas, was the son of a third Nicholas who died intestate in 1649. On the architect's tombstone his age is given as 75. Vertue calls him 'near 70', and at the time of his marriage in 1696 Hawksmoor was described as about 30, but those parish records which survive for 1664–7 do not contain his baptismal entry while those for the four previous years, which may be presumed to do so, are missing.

The extent of his education can only be inferred from his adult familiarity with elementary mathematics, French and Latin and his first known employment as a clerk; the place of his education could have been the grammar school at Dunham, less than two miles from East Drayton. His use of English in later life is assured and easy, though apparently free from purely literary allusions. Most of his known drawing and handwriting dates from after 1688, and both by then show the fluency and discipline of long practice. On the other hand the pages of the sketch-book in the Royal Institute of British Architects of 1680–3 show a scarcely formed writing hand, and a naïve drawing style in which only the selectivity of what is drawn anticipates in any way the future interest and capacity of the student: some of the views have the customary Latin titles of *Ill. 3*

4 Inigo Jones. Greenwich. The Queen's House

5 John Webb. Greenwich Hospital. King Charles Block

topographical prints, and some of the little scenes through doorways are very sensitively drawn. In our age, which offers to youth in general the attention formerly bestowed only on rare prodigies, it is doubly difficult – and no less important – to remember that many artists only mature late and slowly; in Hawksmoor's own century, while the long careers of Bernini and Wren stem from already astonishing achievement in their early teens, Rembrandt or Rubens at the age of twenty had little to show to history beyond raw energy of thought and execution and perhaps – though this is hindsight – promise for the future. Hawksmoor first worked as clerk to Justice Samuel Mellish of Doncaster, who owned property at Dunham and could have known him well already. From Vertue and the obituary we learn that Hawksmoor became Wren's clerk in London at the age of about eighteen, and the plasterer Edward Gouge may have been the link with Wren. However, it is not necessary to suppose that Wren either expected or foresaw in the young man any outstanding talents.

This would have been in 1679–80, twenty years after the Restoration. In London the memory of the Great Fire of 1666 was fading. Wren, in his late forties, was on the plateau of his architectural career; a brick London had risen in place of the wooden city, and among the new churches there already rose

above it the nearly completed steeple of his St Mary-le-Bow and the choir and transept walls of his new St Paul's Cathedral. Whitehall Palace, whose annexes in Scotland Yard included Wren's official residence as Surveyor of the King's Works, still consisted largely of Tudor buildings; the most notable addition was Inigo Jones's Banqueting House, finished in 1622 and Britain's first intelligently and uncompromisingly classical building in the Italian Renaissance sense. At Greenwich, down the river from London, two other landmarks in the history of architecture stood deserted. The Queen's House, also by Jones, had been finished in 1635; it is one of the prototypes of the English country villa, but some of its prestige at the time resulted from its ingenious position astride the Woolwich Road. (It stood in the same relation to the 1680s as another famous bridge-building, the Dessau Bauhaus, stands to the 1960s.) The other building at Greenwich was the unfinished first block of the palace begun for Charles II in 1662 by Jones's pupil Webb. It was fenced around with its windows and doorways boarded up, and few besides Wren can have comprehended its monumental scale and massive solidity. Two decades later it was to form the germ of Greenwich Hospital, with which both Wren and Hawksmoor were concerned, and the latter was to find in the Queen's House an insuperable obstacle to his plans.

Ill. 4

Ill. 5

Domestic architecture was still involved with formulas established by Jones. In suburban Piccadilly, Clarendon House, the large, plain, regular and impeccably finished work of the gentleman architect Roger Pratt, was less than fifteen years old, but was soon to be demolished by a property developer. A hundred yards away the smaller Berkeley House by Hugh May, Comptroller of the King's Works, hinted in its use of brick with stone dressings at May's knowledge of Holland, but gave no inkling of the fully Baroque interiors being completed in the early 1680s under him at Windsor, resplendent in the carving of Grinling Gibbons and the illusionism of the painter Verrio. The most interesting new house in London was the first Montagu House in Bloomsbury, completed in 1679, burnt down seven years later, and designed by Wren's colleague in the sciences and friend in architecture, Dr Robert Hooke. Its distinct Mansard roofs over centre and end pavilions were recognized by contemporaries as strongly French, while the painted interiors were again the work of Verrio.

Wren had been ten when the Civil War broke out, and went up to Oxford in the year of Charles I's execution; his uncle Matthew, Bishop of Ely, was imprisoned for eighteen years for his conformist and royalist beliefs, but many of Christopher's Oxford friends, scientists like himself, were radical in their sympathies. It was as a brilliant science don that Wren, at the age of thirty, turned his hand and mind to designing a building, and it was in the same capacity that he first came to the notice of Charles II; the king's offer of the reversion of the surveyorship at that time was either an unpremeditated gesture or a piece of extraordinary shrewdness. Hawksmoor, a generation later, grew up in an atmosphere of less open conflict between King and Parliament; moreover, he grew up far from London and Westminster. We never hear of his being good at anything except architecture (and talking about it), and while the story of the country boy who becomes a great artist is told of many, from Giotto onwards, the indications are that Hawksmoor was such a country boy, and that many of his ideas and beliefs and much of his character were acquired in his twenties, through his association with Wren and through his reading.

His work for Wren started as that of a personal clerk and continued through a succession of subordinate official appointments, and it is clear from records of things he was paid to do in the 1680s and 1690s that his training included every activity of the architect (or *surveyor*, as he was usually called), every stage of work in the office and on the site. On the evidence of the sketch-book he visited Bath, Bristol and the Midlands in 1680–3. A rereading of the evidence shows the first documentary mention of him to be in January 1684 at Winchester Palace (begun 1682, abandoned 1685) when he witnessed the will of Hugh May; in November 1684 he witnessed a brickmaker's contract there. He appears in the Whitehall accounts (for a time as Henry Hawksmoor) from 1685. In 1687 he was finding stationery for the office dealing with the new London churches, and eight years later he was paid for transcribing its accounts. Meanwhile in 1692 we find him undertaking a commission on the recommendation, and partly still under the name, of Wren: the new Writing School of Christ's Hospital, London (p. 27). He had been made Clerk of Works at the king's new house at Kensington in 1689; the form of payments between 1691 and 1710 at St Paul's implies that he took charge of the drawing office there as one of his activities. In the development of Greenwich Hospital he was Wren's personal clerk for two years before being officially established as Clerk of Works in 1698. Yet also in the 1690s there are several references, some implied but others specific, to Hawksmoor as 'Sir Christopher Wren's gentleman' or as his draughtsman, and he gradually began to receive independent commissions, a practice which was then neither unethical nor unusual for officers of the Crown.

Ill. 13

The libraries of both Wren and Hawksmoor, including many architectural books, were catalogued for sale after death. From the circumstances of sale in each case it is possible that some additional books found their way into the catalogue, but there is a considerable area of similarity between the collections. Moreover, we know that both used books which do not appear in the catalogues, and the extent of their book knowledge is confirmed by their own writings: reports and letters to patrons, and in Wren's case what appear to be drafts for a number of papers or lectures on the theory and history of architecture. Indirect evidence may be added from the many references to books in the diary of Wren's friend Hooke. The latter may have visited Holland; Hugh May went there and probably to France also. Wren visited France in 1665–6 and significantly declared his intention of bringing back 'almost all France in paper'. He never went abroad again and Hawksmoor never went at all. They thus depended for knowledge of European architecture on the word of others and on written, drawn and printed matter. In the English Baroque school of the late seventeenth and early eighteenth centuries, as in the Roman Baroque school of the first half of the seventeenth, energy went predominantly into the production of works and only minimally into theoretical writing: this is in contrast to the Palladian movement which began, and continued after 1715, with an unprecedented crop of illustrative, didactic and theoretical publications. Although Wren and Hooke appear to have considered sponsoring an English version of Perrault's 1673 edition of Vitruvius nothing came of it, and books were, for Wren and his circle, sources of information and sometimes of justification or rationalization for ideas empirically conceived.

The books available to Hawksmoor in the 1680s included both the treatises of the revival of ancient architecture and illustrations of its practical results in Renaissance Italy. There were also in growing numbers works on seventeenth-century buildings, both in Italy and in France and the Netherlands – buildings based like his own on an assimilation and a freer interpretation of the Renaissance. St Peter's and other great Roman churches from the time of Bramante to that of Bernini and Borromini, the new buildings of the Louvre, the châteaux and town houses of seventeenth-century France, the new Town

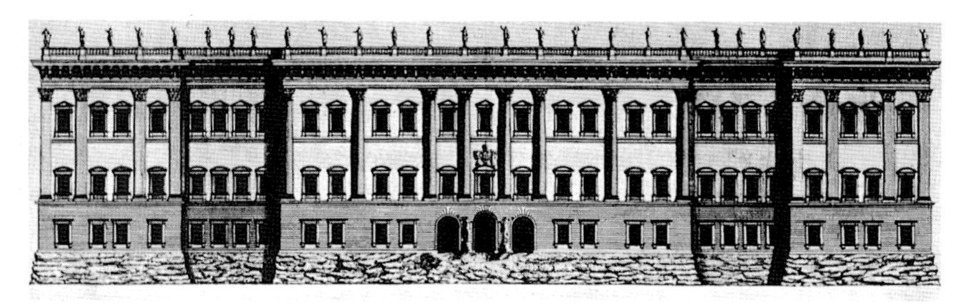

6 Bernini. Third Project for the east front of the Louvre. 1665

Hall of Amsterdam and some at least of the Dutch churches, were all potentially as familiar in fine engravings as the crude wood-block exemplars of Serlio and the more refined details of Palladio and Scamozzi. Wren moreover maintained, and transmitted to Hawksmoor, an interest in the more exotic styles of Asia Minor and in the scanty literature on Greece and Egypt. In England the beginnings of antiquarianism and the growth of skill in engraving combined to provide illustrations of many native medieval buildings, and while Wren may have labelled Gothic as an occasional deviation from a 'better' style Hawksmoor stands, with his Austrian contemporary Fischer von Erlach, among the first architects with a real interest in the history of architecture and in the discrimination of styles.

The Wren school's receptivity to a wide variety of influences, and its conscious attitude to styles as if they were garments in which to clothe buildings, were in part due to the progress of engraving as an accurate and detailed means of reproducing buildings and designs. But it should not be imagined that this eclectic attitude to style resulted from, or even accompanied, a stylelessness in the architects; nor are the changes in their style simply changes from one source to another, even though Wren, for instance, became gradually more attuned to Italian Baroque as against French influences. Wren's use of the giant order, two storeys high, becomes more frequent in design and more assured in handling during the 1680s. When he saw the drawings for Bernini's great project for the Louvre in 1665 he was so impressed and moved that he would have 'given my skin' to have them, but it seems as if the implications of classical

Ill. 6

architecture on so monumental a scale were not fruitful until his intellect had come, over a period of years, to accept what his eye had told him in that brief inspection. Similarly, though he knew something of Borromini's use of curved surfaces in walls and towers by the 1680s it is only a decade later that his general prejudice in favour of straight lines allowed him to combine convex and concave shapes in some of the late church steeples. Hawksmoor, who entertained the same prejudice, was nevertheless able to assimilate Borrominesque forms more directly and to reinterpret them in angular terms. *Ill. 109*

Wren's mind was finely balanced between cogitation and inspiration. In science, he was capable of devising the theoretical formula to solve a problem but not bothering to proceed to the solution; on the other hand he found congenial the emphasis of post-Baconian science on experiment, because he needed visible results to maintain his interest. This need may explain his involvement first with anatomy and then with architecture. He was convinced of the mathematical basis of the whole of creation and therefore of the dependence of beauty on geometry, but at the same time he admitted a second order of 'customary' or associative beauty. In architecture, his solids and spaces convey an innate feeling for solid geometry which is as much a mathematician's as the 'feeling' some have for numbers. He was usually ready to temper aesthetic rules by consideration of the total visual effect, and on occasion said so. The recognition of associative beauty is related to the acceptance we find, in drawings and the development of designs, of experiment in visual terms.

Hawksmoor took over, to an extent that indicates not only discipleship but a natural sympathy, the geometrical feeling of Wren's architecture. This is the one characteristic of their work that neither committed to words, and which the pure-form aesthetic of a later age has enabled us better to appreciate and to describe. In a letter of 1724 answering Palladian criticism, Hawksmoor described the bases of his art as he saw them, equating the 'Rules of the Ancients' of his critics with 'Strong

Reason and good fancy, joyn'd with experience and tryalls, so that we are assured of the good effect of it'. *Reason* is related both to seventeenth-century French academic theory and to Wren's emphasis on mathematics and intellect. *Fancy*, or imagination, is a quality of which Wren was avowedly wary, since it 'blinds the judgement'; it is necessarily opposed to reason and he was only prepared to admit it in the heavily rationalized guise of empirical experiment, that procedure which Hawksmoor called *experience and trials*.

The place of Fancy in Hawksmoor's work is self-evident; its importance in his attitude to art, in contrast to Wren's, is probably due directly or indirectly to the writings of Thomas Hobbes, the materialist philosopher who died in 1679 at the age of 91. Hobbes produced, incidentally in *Leviathan* (1651) and more centrally in the *Answer to Davenant* (1650), the closest approach before Coleridge to a psychology of the imagination. Among the concepts he discussed was one of particular relevance to the evocative power we discern in Hawksmoor's architecture: the effect of works of art on the emotions without the intermediacy of intellect. Whether or not Hawksmoor read Hobbes is not very material. The concept of archetypes is today familiar to many people who have not read Jung. One tends to underestimate the extent of knowledge where it is not recorded: to take an example from Hawksmoor's youth, the sash window came into prominence for the first time, yet we have very little evidence about its invention, and no literary evidence at all.

Wren's was the most important personal influence on the younger architect, and the easiest to define. It is more difficult to discuss Hawksmoor's relation to William Talman, who remains a mysterious figure in spite of a good deal of documentation. Talman was born in 1650. On 2 May 1689 he was appointed by William III to the Comptrollership of Works (second to the Surveyor) which had been vacant for the five years since the death of May; soon after the accession of Queen Anne in 1702 he was deprived in favour of Vanbrugh. On

7 William Talman. Chatsworth. South front

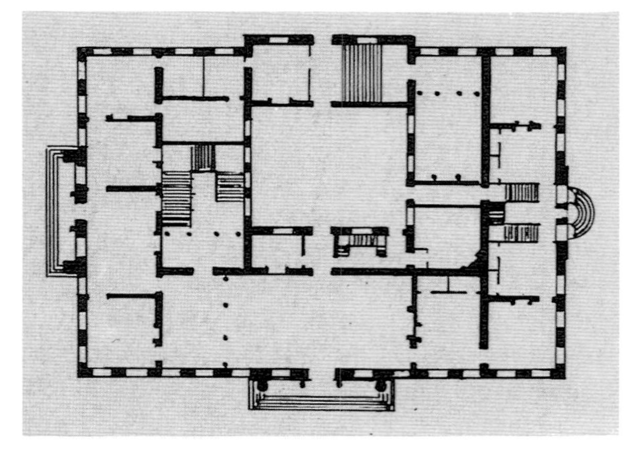

8 William Talman. Thoresby (destroyed). Plan

9 Easton Neston. East front

Vanbrugh's evidence and from other sources he was clearly arrogant, and lost a number of patrons in the middle of commissions; it was in this way that at an early stage he lost Castle Howard to Vanbrugh (p. 47). The sequence in office of May, Talman and Vanbrugh, all interested in country house design, may be fortuitous, although Talman was probably May's pupil and Wren was patently not committed to this branch of architecture. With the south front of Chatsworth, begun in *Ill. 7* 1687, Talman introduced into English domestic architecture the giant pilaster order and rectangular silhouette which were to contribute a few years later to the monumentality of Hawksmoor's Easton Neston (p. 34). Another aspect of *Ill. 9* Talman's work is often underrated because so much was destroyed or never executed: the use of sequences of rooms, of internal screens of pillars and of open-well staircases for varied and unexpected spatial effects. Whether he can have influenced Hawksmoor directly must depend on when they first met. Hawksmoor may have seen Talman's first great house, Thoresby, Notts under construction in the mid 1680s, for he *Ill. 8* wrote of it much later in terms which could imply inside

knowledge. The question of Talman's relation to the origins of Easton Neston is involved in itself, but a project by Hawksmoor for Ingestre Hall dated 1688 – and thus early in Talman's architectural career and before his Works appointment – shows equal spatial ingenuity. The key on the plan shows that the vestibule (B) was to be twenty feet (one storey) high and separated by column-screens from spaces of twice that height, the hall (A) and staircase (C). The staircase appears (though the evidence for one flight consists of pencil lines and probability) to be of the form beloved by German Baroque designers and known as the imperial, with a single central first flight leading through turns of 180 degrees to two parallel upper flights. The upper landing was thus in the centre of the house over the vestibule, possibly with windows or arches looking down into the hall. The upper rooms over the gallery were reached from it; the wings had separate staircases.

Ill. 10

An altogether larger and more difficult question is whether, and if so when, Hawksmoor's style began to influence that of his master Wren. His hand is not to be seen in any of the projects for Hampton Court. At St Paul's, where it may be distinguished in some of the later drawings, we know in any case of his connections with the drawing office. His responsibility for parts of Greenwich Hospital rests on quite different evidence (p. 46). These questions involve documents and drawings, which often do not tell us what we most want to know; they involve considerations of artistic style and the probabilities of human behaviour; sometimes they involve the hazards of purely negative evidence. To some extent the answers we are able to discover depend not on evidence at all but on *a priori* ideas of the artistic personality. The romantic idea of the genius who does everything with his own hands is inappropriate to an architect's office, or any other in which delegation of work and responsibility is natural. But the fragmentation of a previously accepted whole personality into the work of assistants is a procedure, by no means unknown, which reduces scholarly analysis to a parody. There is also a

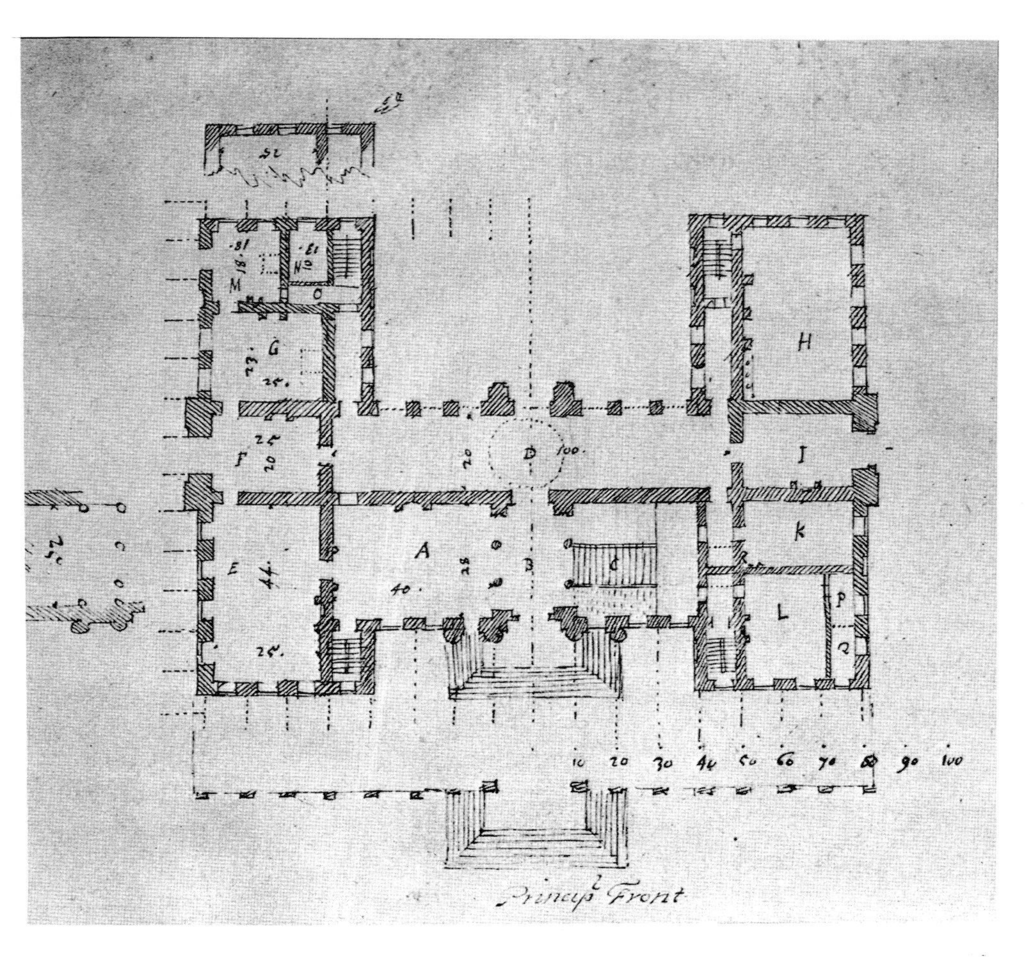

10 Project for 'Villa Chetwiniana', Ingestre

natural human interest in tales of mistaken identity and unrecognized genius. In many individual matters we shall never know the precise extent of Hawksmoor's responsibility, but the picture of his work presented in the following pages is based on the assumption that an artistic personality, from the very fact that it has solidity and depth, presents both a consistent core and a variety of individual facets.

CHAPTER TWO

Practice

Wren's unexecuted first Hampton Court project of 1689 exemplifies the greater monumentality he attained during the preceding decade and continued to develop in the following one, towards the 1698 scheme for Whitehall Palace. The emergence of Hawksmoor as an autonomous artist during the 1690s appears, from the surviving drawings, to be a quite distinct process. He did some work at Broadfield Hall, near Buntingford, in 1690–3, but little is known about it though it probably included interior alterations and the design of the stable wing. With the Writing School at Christ's Hospital, built 1692–5, we are on firmer, though still distant, ground. The school, which was demolished in 1902, was a plain brick and stone building of which Wren was nominally in charge. However, Hawksmoor received a gratuity and a vote of thanks so worded that it is clear that he both designed the school and supervised its execution. The preliminary drawings in the Wren collection at All Souls, which are in his hand, show a more striking building than that carried out, and one quite different from anything by Wren. The school room was upstairs, over a stone arcade of three bays by five, which originally contained shops whose rent was to pay for the upkeep of the school. The drawings show a building large in scale rather than in size – 45 feet high – conceived in few large units. The effect of a giant order is achieved not by using one but by implying it in the corner projections and the big brick parapet and stone cornice and coping. The almost total absence of decoration, the concentration on bare rather than modulated surfaces, and the use of windows and storeys larger than in the schoolmaster's house at the corner, are all devices to impress us with the bigness of the building. The addition of the pretty

Ill. 14

Ill. 12

Ill. 13

11 Vanbrugh and Hawksmoor. Castle Howard. The hall

lead cupolas on the end pavilions is the stroke of genius that would have prevented the school from looking like a factory.

In 1697 Hawksmoor received a similar gratuity 'for Coppy designes and Papers by Sr. Chr. Wrens orders' in connection with the rebuilding of the tower and nave of St Mary's, Warwick, ruined by fire in September 1694. It seems to have been accepted that the rebuilding should be in a 'Gothick' style sympathetic to the remaining eastern part of the church. The design of a local architect was finally chosen, but besides the payment and some other documentary mentions there is evidence from sketches that Hawksmoor was concerned in the preliminary stages. They include a perspective which

12 Detail of Wren's project for Whitehall, 1698

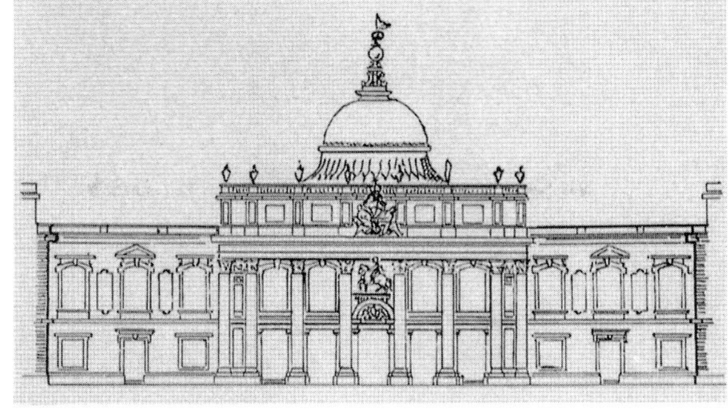

14 Wren's project for Hampton Court, 1689. Detail of west front

reduces to essentials both the medieval work and his own design for tower, nave and transepts. The grey wash which is the greater part of the drawing describes a building essentially the same as the Writing School: large masses boldly defined by horizontal and vertical lines, and made fully plastic by the selective emphasis of highlights and shadows. The linear patterns and complexities of Gothic architecture did not concern him. Yet because he conceived all buildings in terms of masses and cavities and observed the way light falls and casts shadows on them, he came nearer to the nature of Gothic than most of the eighteenth-century gothicizers and nearer than the faintly pencilled details of mouldings and tracery on

Ill. 15

13 Design for end elevation, Christ's Hospital Writing School

15 Project for St Mary, Warwick

16 Project for St Augustine, Watling Street

17 Kensington Palace. King's Gallery

the drawing might suggest by themselves. Later on he was to demonstrate more clearly the transmutability of his architecture from one style to another. *Ills. 106, 109*

Another drawing of the early 1690s, a project for the steeple of St Augustine, Watling Street, is done in pencil and wash, with alternative corner pinnacles. In a second autograph version the openwork finial and other protrusions are coloured yellow to suggest gilding. His fondness for wash as something more than diagrammatic colouring, for the drawing as a picture which stands up out of the page, never left him. *Ill. 16*

As Clerk of Works at Kensington, Hawksmoor was instrumental from the outset in 1689 in the conversion of the Jacobean Nottingham House into a suburban palace for William III, who found the damp air of Whitehall uncongenial. Wren, and probably Talman, were concerned with this task which the king pressed forward with an urgency and an inconstancy that ruled out any integrated planning. Most of the work is

domestic in scale; the chief exception is the last block to be constructed, the King's Gallery (begun 1695). The giant pilaster strips and heavy attic of this front speak again, almost entirely in terms of red and orange brick, the plain monumental language of the Christ's Hospital Writing School, and on this evidence it is to be presumed Hawksmoor's work. The bracketed wooden cornice originally had the metopes 'finished, or enricht' but in 1717 it was painted a uniform colour as it is today.

Ill. 17

For Hawksmoor's most important commission of this period, Easton Neston, there are virtually no drawings and no documents. Because of its significance both architecturally and in Hawksmoor's development it is necessary to state in some detail the known facts and the most reasonable conclusions to be drawn from them. The commission to build a new country house for Sir William Fermor evidently came once more through Wren, who was distantly related to Fermor by marriage. Two letters from Wren to Fermor exist: one is datable 1687, the other, without year, expresses the hope that 'you provide to carry up one storey of the great house next yeare'. John Bridges's *History of Northamptonshire*, compiled from notes after his death in 1724, attributes the wings to Wren and dates them 'about twenty years' before the main house in which 'Hawkesmore . . . hath very much departed from the first design'. The date 1702, which Bridges gives for the completion, appears on the garden front and on rainwater heads. On his evidence the wings, of which only the north one survives, were begun in the early 1680s under Wren – if perhaps not *by* him. The distance between them of about 125 feet limited the width of any future main building; the house is at the top of a slight rise, well to the north of the previous mansion, and the drainage of the site and alignment of the forecourt axis on Greens Norton church in the distance were undertaken with evident care. One of the three drawings possibly connected with the house is concerned with levels and is inscribed by Hawksmoor 'July 23. 1686. Memdm for Easton. To make the Grasse on the Garden Side 4 fot deep from the top of the Water table'. A water-table in the architectural sense is a ledge sloping outwards at the base of a wall, and the mention of the garden side implies that the wall in question was that of the 'great house'. The further implications are that Wren's undated letter to Fermor was written in 1685 or 1686, and that by the latter year he had turned part or all of the work over to Hawksmoor.

Ill. 9

Ill. 18

The wooden model at Easton Neston represents a house clearly divided horizontally into two storeys, with no giant order, but conforming with the building in two important respects: the breaking forward of the main elevations towards the centre (a common Baroque means of introducing movement to a façade) and the disposition of the interior. The 'first design' mentioned by Bridges must, however, have preceded the model by some years, as its origins lie in a drawing for a house in Wren's hand at All Souls. Both Wren and later

18 The model for Easton Neston

Hawksmoor wrote of the wings as if they were by someone else, and the All Souls drawing, which has pitched roofs and a lantern, was certainly never executed. But another design came between this and the model.

Some time in the 1690s Thomas Colepeper made rough copies of drawings for a more modern house with a flat top, which has some of the final internal features but not yet the remarkable hall and staircase which appear first in the model and again in the house itself. If building to this design was ever begun, it cannot have proceeded very far, for the structure of the final house is notably homogeneous. It seems probable that Sir William Fermor originally asked Wren's advice in the early 1680s but did not use his design for the wings, that Hawksmoor was involved by 1686, and that there was then a long pause. Fermor married his second wife in 1682, perhaps at the time the wings were begun; she died in 1687. It is probable that the incentive and the material opportunity for the main house came from Fermor's acquisition in 1692 of the Barony of Lempster, the hand in marriage of Sophia Osborne, daughter of the Earl of Danby (later Duke of Leeds) and a dowry reported by Narcissus Luttrell to be £10,000. It is evident from the

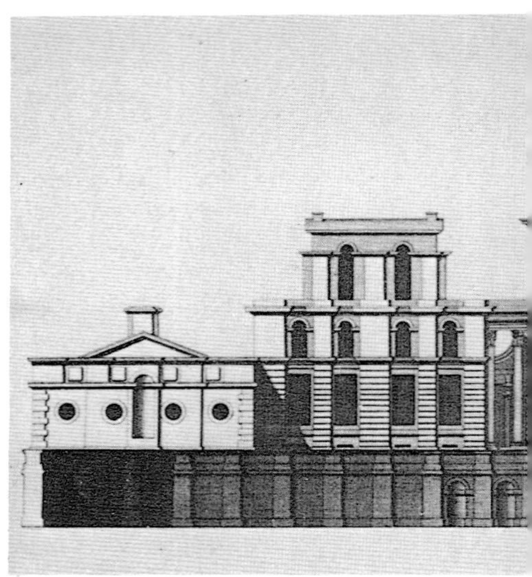

19 Project for Easton Neston (*Vitruvius Britannicus*, 1715)

Ill. 10 Ingestre project of 1688 that Hawksmoor could have designed a house of such spatial complexity and dramatic inventiveness as early as the late 1680s. Nevertheless both stylistic analysis and the sparse documentation point to a starting date for the main house of around 1694, when a proper and very skilfully engineered water supply was laid on to the site from a point over a mile away. The model must be earlier than 1694; it represents a squatter, perhaps a brick, house without a giant order. In recent years the idea has spread that Easton Neston is somehow Wren's design; however, in a letter of 1731 after a visit to the house Hawksmoor wrote of it that 'one can hardly avoy'd loveing ones owne children' and this by itself ought to be enough to establish that he was responsible for its design. He also called the wings 'good for nothing', a comment which he is unlikely to have made about a work of his revered master, but which may reflect his failure to interest the second Lord Lempster, who succeeded in 1711, in recasing them and adding *Ill. 19* a cupola as shown in the plate in *Vitruvius Britannicus* (Vol. I, 1715).

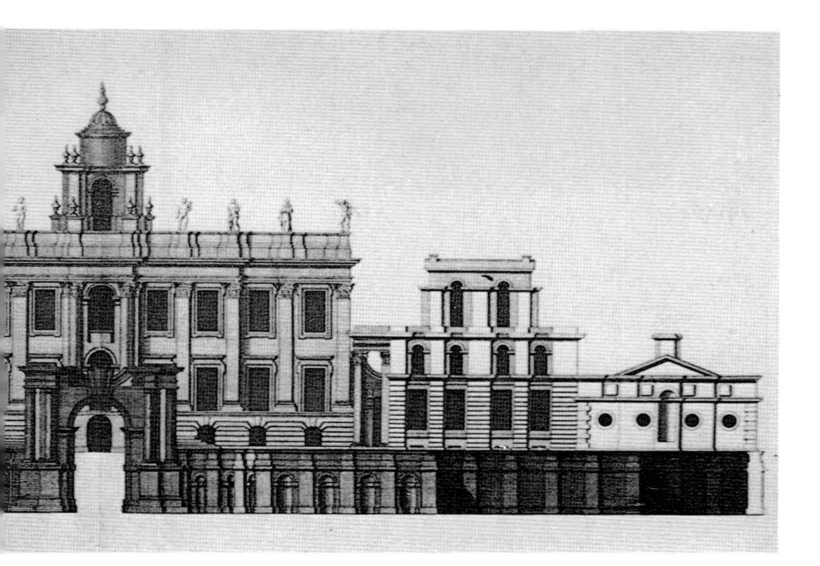

Easton Neston has a tallness fairly unusual for England in comparison, for example, with Chatsworth. The close spacing of the order, which reinforces this tallness, occurs, moreover, elsewhere in Hawksmoor's œuvre: for example the one-and-a-half-diameter intercolumniations, at the end of his career, which he brought both structural and aesthetic reasons to defend in the Mausoleum at Castle Howard. The centrewards movement of the Easton Neston façade is enriched by subtle variations in bay width, those at the ends being slightly wider. Hawksmoor's habit of changing his mind, the practice recorded at Greenwich Hospital and at Blenheim of hoisting up full-size models of details and ornaments to assess their effect, and the apparently casual approach which the correspondence about the Mausoleum reveals (p. 199) towards fruitful accidents in invention, should not be allowed to obscure the amount of attention he paid to subtleties and small details in the final design. The instruction written on a plan for a copyist, to 'keep the angles sharp' and his concern in his Worcester College designs with specific prototypes for details (p. 149), are

Ill. 159

reflections of the exactness and sharpness of the detail of Easton Neston.

In 1691 Fermor (as he then was) bought the Arundel collection of antique marble statues which are now in the Ashmolean at Oxford. He died before arranging them to his satisfaction, and a visitor in the middle of the eighteenth century found marbles everywhere and nobody who could explain them to him. Fermor's intention of making his new house a sculpture museum in the tradition of Arundel, the Humanists and the Romans, seems to be reflected in and thus to explain the austere character of the interior, especially what we know of the original appearance of the hall. This room originally ran from the centre bay of the house to the south end; the end bays were one storey high and the middle section was twice the height with a shallow unlit dome. In the late nineteenth century a floor was inserted to make the upper part into an extra bedroom and the northern end of the hall was partitioned off and opened on the other side to make a new entrance hall. The drawing given here [Ill. 21] is a schematic reconstruction of the original arrangement. Although Hawksmoor's introduction of the front door into the side of one end of the hall recalls the traditional plan of medieval and Tudor houses, his purpose seems to have been neither

Ill. 22

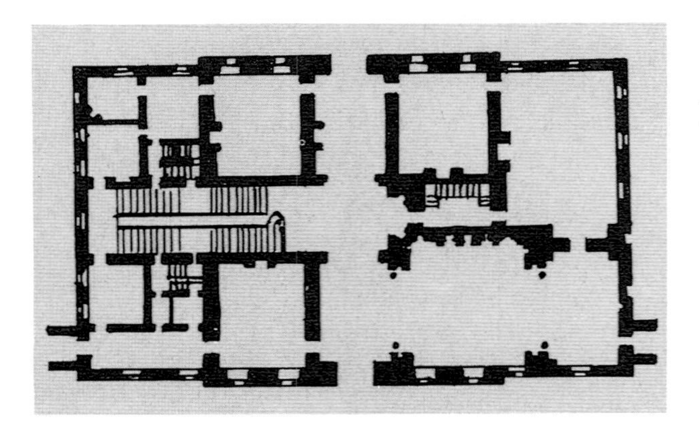

20 Easton Neston. Original plan of main block

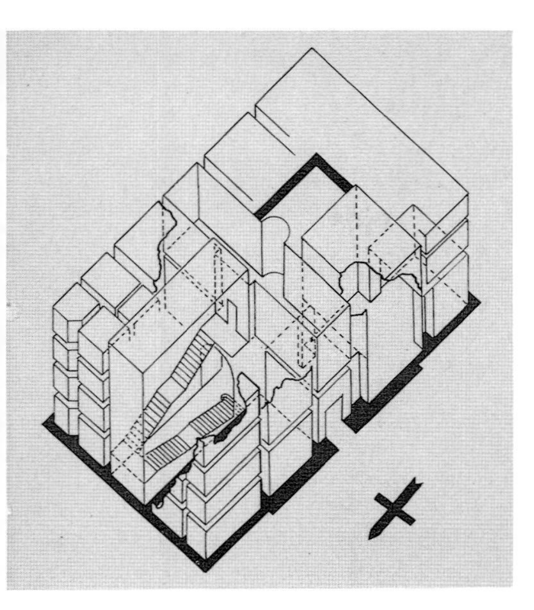

21 Easton Neston.
Isometric diagram of the interior

22 Easton Neston.
The hall before alteration

functional nor antiquarian. Both at Easton Neston and in the Ingestre project it was spatial, the interior organization of Easton Neston being the more elaborate. There is something of a young man's bravado in the skill and effectiveness with which he packs rooms of state and accommodation into this block, relatively small as great houses go. Each of the two northern corners has its own staircase, and by the use of mezzanines each contains four floors instead of two; each of the three upper floors has a bedroom suite, and the corners are in effect the *pavillons* of a French great house embedded within the silhouette of a single block. At the south end there is only an upper mezzanine. The rest of the house is taken up by large rooms of full height and by the hall and staircase.

The visitor enters (or did originally) to find the long and major axis of the hall at right angles to his line of travel. If he does not turn right into the middle of the hall but continues straight ahead he comes to the foot of the staircase, whose

23 Easton Neston. Gallery niche

24 Easton Neston. Staircase

axis is again at right angles but this time to the left. The stair cage rises the full height of the house between the two embedded *pavillons*. He can either proceed through to the rooms of the garden front or turn left up the staircase, turning right about at the half landing and reaching the upper floor directly above the stair foot. The gallery ahead (now, and perhaps always screened from the staircase and reached through a small rectangular door) presents a further right-angle change of direction, running across the axis on which he entered the house and giving access to the main rooms on the upper floor.

Ill. 20

Ill. 24

Ill. 23

Hawksmoor's powers of spatial manipulation are best shown in the staircase; this long tall narrow space has to be traversed twice through its length in order to rise half its height, to the top landing. The ascent is so gradual and the steps are so

25 Easton Neston. Staircase

26 Easton Neston. West and north fronts

broad that the visitor is compelled, physically and psychologically, to travel slowly either upwards or downwards – and thus to experience to the full his changing position within its limits. The light, which comes entirely from the large north window, enhances his experience by first intruding on him to the point of obscuring details, and then illuminating details superbly when he turns away from the light.

Ill. 25

The long elevations have two rows of large windows and the short south front is three windows high because of the mezzanine; the north front combines a two- with a four-storey elevation. This lack of consistency reflects and can be explained by, but is not logically necessitated by, the ingenious arrangement of the interior. For the relation of inside and outside at the north end is still inexact and partly arbitrary:

Ill. 26

some of the big corner windows light – and conceal – the small rooms and intermediate floors. While it may be that the interior was the starting point for the exterior (for which Hawksmoor could have offered the precedent of Ammanati's Collegio Romano in Rome) its logic is entirely one of visual patterning. Large and small windows, round and angular forms make a counterpoint of several different themes. When the basis of these differences within one front is understood, the differences between adjacent fronts hardly require comment; in any case the example of Chatsworth and those houses which derive from it make such differences into something like a stylistic principle in English Baroque country houses.

Ill. 27 Stylistically it is a small step from the north front of Easton Neston to the court elevation of King William Block at Greenwich Hospital. Hawksmoor's initial connection with the Hospital (the naval counterpart of Chelsea and now the Royal Naval College) has been mentioned (p. 15); he was to

27 Greenwich Hospital. King William Block. East front

28 Greenwich Hospital from the north

be Assistant Surveyor from 1705 to 1729 and Clerk of Works until 1733 when he was shabbily suspended, with the humiliation of being paid an annuity of £50 by Thomas Ripley. The great extension schemes for which he made drawings belong to a later chapter (p. 96); for his authorship of executed buildings there is no documentary proof. He viewed Greenwich with obvious parental affection and also with no little frustration as, under the inadequate provision of successive governments and finally under the alien hands of Ripley and other new Palladian officers of the Works, he saw it sink from a 'publick Building' to a 'deformed Barrac'. His feelings are stated in letters to Lord Carlisle; they are implied in the *Remarks* he published on the building in 1728, but he says very little about designs either executed or projected. As Wren's clerk he was preparing drawings in 1696–7 and for those parts of the Hospital in which Wren's authorship is undisputed: the complex of hall, chapel and colonnades which face each other across the strip of land on the central axis between the Queen's House and the Thames. The essence of *Ill. 29*

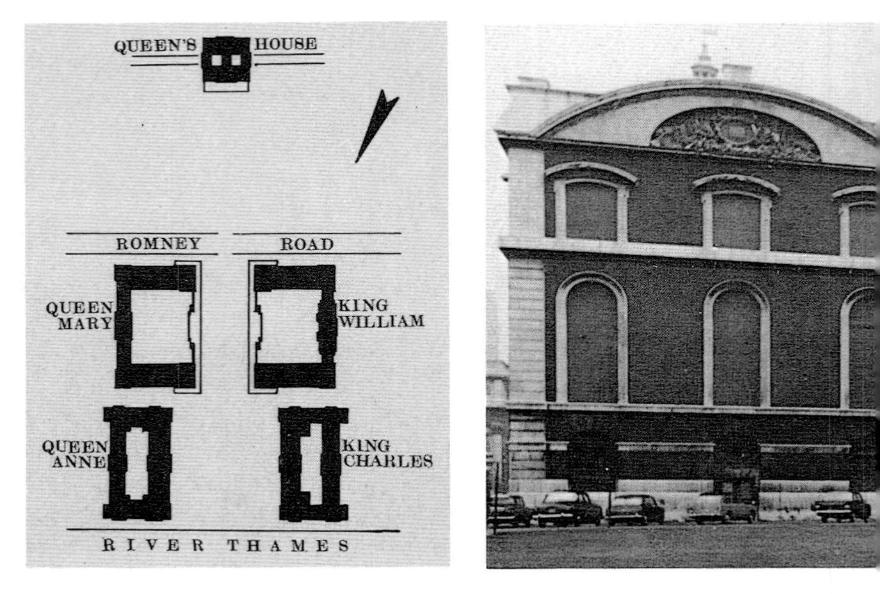

29 Greenwich Hospital. Plan

30 Greenwich Hospital. Queen Anne Block. East front

31 Greenwich Hospital. King William Block. West front

the Greenwich problem was the fact that the royal grant of the estate of Greenwich Palace in 1694 did not include this central strip, and Greenwich was thus doomed to be a building without a middle. Wren's final solution was to develop the Hospital in four blocks, incorporating the north-west range built and the north-east one planned by Webb for Charles II, and framing the Queen's House vista with the colonnades and domed vestibules of the hall and chapel. A study of the building accounts reveals at least the dates of the various buildings, and establishes that the base block at the back of the north-east range (Queen Anne Block) was begun in 1700 while the middle of King William Block was begun in 1699 and most of its carcass and external decoration was up early in 1702. It is in these buildings that a style appears that is different from either Wren's earlier work or the Whitehall designs of 1698. The Queen Anne façade, which from its location contemporaries would have called a 'backfront', carries on the style of the Writing School, but in stone its bareness is the more evident.

Ill. 28

Ill. 30

Ills. 27, 31

Ill. 13

The brick and stone fronts of the King William Building display a freedom, even a competent wildness, in the use of scale and pattern which it is hard to imagine were due to Wren. The Surveyor of Works was still capable at over seventy of designing the dome and west towers of St Paul's. Greenwich was the greatest secular building he was likely to achieve, and one in which he took considerable personal interest, and it seems unlikely that in his late sixties he would readily have delegated any major portion of it even to so trusted an assistant as Hawksmoor. Nevertheless this seems the least unreasonable interpretation of the evidence. We see the language of classical architecture across not only the Renaissance but also the suavity of Georgian Palladianism, the scholarliness of neo-classicism, systematic archaeology and the architectural academies. There is some evidence at the time that, in spite of an often learned concern for detailing and a practical familiarity with the classical vocabulary, Wren's contemporaries were a good deal less sophisticated than later generations about the ways in which they could employ it. Wren may well have been liberal enough to commend the interplay of windows and gable shapes in King William Block, the tall western portico that supports only an enormous plinth, the half-oval triumphal arch on the court side and the stilted aedicule within it whose stilts at least derive from designs of his own.

The relatively early date of this block effectively rules out the participation, which used to be assumed, of Vanbrugh (p. 9). Through the influence of the third Earl of Carlisle he replaced Talman as Comptroller of Works on 18 June 1702; this was too late to influence in any official way the design of the block, and he did not attend the Greenwich Directors' meetings until October 1703. In the forty years since the first important studies of the 'Vanbrugh school' our knowledge of the respective roles of Vanbrugh and Hawksmoor has greatly increased and the balance has changed. It is now clear that Hawksmoor's inventive activity precedes Vanbrugh's by a decade, that Easton Neston does not depend on Vanbrugh, and that the latter's approach to architecture was basically simple whereas Hawksmoor's may fairly be called basically complex. Vanbrugh was born in 1664; in 1686 he became a professional soldier though it would be more just to call him an amateur. In 1690 he was in France as a civilian and was imprisoned for two years as a spy – probably as a hostage for exchange with a French agent. It is presumed that he cast an interested eye on French architecture before his arrest – it is not unknown nowadays for architectural historians to be arrested on suspicion of espionage – but the proximate result of his experience was his emergence as a writer of 'Restoration' comedies. Nothing has so far been discovered to connect him with architecture before 1699, and the letter dated Christmas Day of that year, which raises the curtain to us half-way through the first act of the story of Castle Howard, induces the same breathless surprise that Swift epitomized for contemporaries (*Van's Genius without Thought or Lecture / Is hugely turnd to Architecture).* Indeed the commencement of the house seems to have been hasty: Hawksmoor expressed himself in 1701 as wishing 'for the conclusion of the worke as earnestly as I was for opposing the beginning of it'. We know that Charles Howard, third Earl of Carlisle, eight years younger than Hawksmoor and five younger than Vanbrugh, first approached Talman for a design, found him difficult to deal with, and seems to have allowed his personal friend Vanbrugh to cut his artistic teeth on the problem. We know from Vanbrugh's Christmas letter that the previous summer, after inspecting the site, he had been looking at Thoresby, Kiveton and Chatsworth, all Talman houses; that many people had seen the designs for Castle Howard and that a wooden model was being made and was to be shown to William III. We know from other sources that the extant preparatory elevations for the house, though not the plans, are in Hawksmoor's hand, that by 1700 Hawksmoor had been suggested by Vanbrugh to Carlisle as a man of experience in dealing with builders and craftsmen, and that by 1706 he had made several journeys to the site and was concerned with the fitting up of the east wing. A review of Vanbrugh's activities shows that when, after war and the stage, he found his true profession in architecture, he took it seriously and with much hard work. His ideas were simple and grand, and he believed that great architecture, exceeding in every way the products of the absolutist king Louis XIV and his minister Colbert, could be realized also under the constitutional monarchy of Whig liberty. It was through no lack of effort of his that, except for the special case of Blenheim, Hampton Court and Greenwich were the last great public commissions for over half a century. But in 1699–1700 he seems to have had ideas and a patron and little else. Hawksmoor, whom he may have met through his cousin William, secretary to Greenwich Hospital, could provide what he lacked: a draughtsman, an administrator and an expert on detail.

The plan and elevation of Castle Howard illustrate this partnership in both the early and the final stages. The interior of the main block is simply planned, with the entrance hall on the main axis flanked by staircases and leading into a one-storey saloon overlooking the garden; the saloon was gutted by fire in 1940 and with it the second saloon above it. The hall-saloon axis probably derives from the villa plans of Palladio, a French edition of whose *Architettura* Vanbrugh described in terms of a compendium of house plans; the double saloon is a common feature of palaces in Central Europe at this time. Other elements of the house are less obviously accounted for. Quite new features of the plan are the long low wings on the garden front and the corridor running through them and the centre of the house. The corridor, which we treat as an obvious necessity in large buildings, appears to have been used only twice before in houses: by Roger Pratt about 1650 at Coleshill and by an unknown architect (Hooke?) at Burley-on-the-Hill, which Vanbrugh saw, still unfinished, on his 1699 tour. The Castle Howard corridor, moreover, offers not merely a device

Ill. 34

Ill. 35

32 Early design for north front, Castle Howard

33 Vanbrugh and Hawksmoor. Castle Howard. North front

35 Vanbrugh and Hawksmoor.
Castle Howard. South front

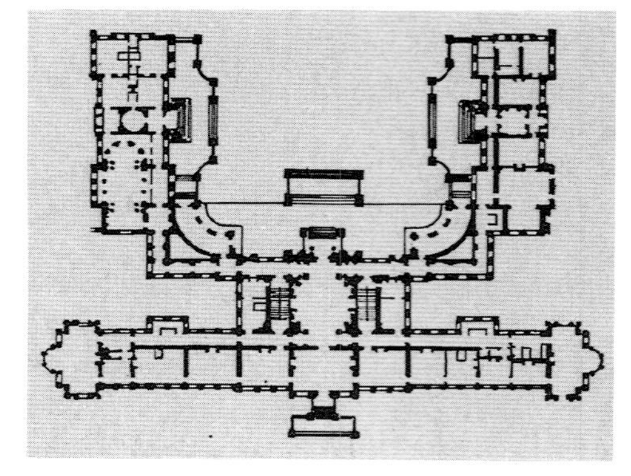

34 Castle Howard.
Plan of main house as in
Vitruvius Britannicus, 1715

of convenience but a tunnel-like vista with dramatic qualities.

Ill. 32 The early elevations are similar to those of Easton Neston; that for the entrance front has the varied rhythm of Hawksmoor's houses but the garden side has the round-headed *Ill. 35* windows of several later Vanbrugh houses. The dome which *Ill. 11* crowns the elevation and lights the hall, was missing from the earliest designs; in one of the plans the supporting piers are added as an afterthought, possibly during 1700. The use of a roof-top cupola as the main light source of such an interior space probably derives from May's Queen's Staircase at Windsor (destroyed *c.* 1800). A further afterthought is the addition of the pediment to the garden front, which is just

late enough to make probable its derivation from the west front of Chatsworth, begun in 1700. It is likely that the unusual or innovatory features of Castle Howard were due to Vanbrugh rather than to Hawksmoor, and that much of the detail – especially inside – was designed by the craftsmen who carried it out. Hawksmoor's contributions to the house were initially less obvious, though he was later to play a major role in the garden buildings. The greatest results for him of the Castle Howard connection were to be the Mausoleum in his last period (p. 198) and, more directly and overlapping in time the building of Vanbrugh's first great house, his share in the second: Blenheim.

Ill. 159

CHAPTER THREE

Apostolate

The grant of Woodstock Park and the construction of a house were the reward of a grateful nation to the Duke of Marlborough for his achievements against the French which culminated in his victory at Blindheim in Bavaria on 13 August 1704. Blenheim was therefore no ordinary house, but a public monument occasioned by an extraordinary event. To Vanbrugh and the Duke it was a monument to British military greatness; in later years, when the Marlboroughs had lost Queen Anne's favour, the Treasury had failed to pay the workmen, and Vanbrugh had resigned after provocation from the Duchess, the latter did her best to make the palace at once a habitable home and a personal monument to the Duke's genius (p. 184). Amid the frayed tempers, broken promises and unroofed galleries it then appeared that very little had been committed to paper in the early days of national enthusiasm and limitless royal bounty; Vanbrugh was lucky to have obtained from Lord Treasurer Godolphin, with extraordinary foresight, a letter of appointment as architect. The choice had been made by Marlborough who was, like Carlisle, his personal friend; Blenheim was not the official responsibility of the Office of Works, but like St Paul's Cathedral it acquired an administration which was a small replica of the Works. It was convenient that Vanbrugh had in 1702 become Comptroller of Works, and it would have been natural for Hawksmoor to act officially as Assistant Surveyor for Blenheim, even without the background of his assistance at Castle Howard. Most of the drawings are again in his hand; there are some references to their joint responsibility for works and designs at Blenheim, and many details of the building are attributable to Hawksmoor. We also have both sides of a correspondence

Ill. 37

36 Blenheim. Tower of kitchen court

37 Vanbrugh and Hawksmoor. Blenheim Palace. North front

between him and Henry Joynes, a young man who first appeared as a lad of about seventeen, looking after stores at Kensington in 1700. Joynes became an able draughtsman, was appointed Clerk of Works at Blenheim, and succeeded Hawksmoor at Kensington after 1715. Hawksmoor's letters give instructions for the conduct of the building; he writes with paternal affection and sometimes offers advice such as that to 'keep your self out of Idle Company', especially at Oxford.

It is easy to imagine that Hawksmoor's attitude in the correspondence was founded on, and reflected, the training and advice he had received in his own early days from Wren. Lofty associations never turned Hawksmoor's head; he always remained a deferential correspondent even to a peer as sympathetic as Lord Carlisle. He seems to have been most at home with masons like the Peisleys and Townesends at Oxford and the Ettys at York: his success in treating with craftsmen

38 Vanbrugh. Water tower on Kensington Palace Green

39 Henry Joynes. Carshalton. Water Pavilion

must have rested on their respect for his professionalism and knowledge and on his recognition of their experience and their personal worth. Joynes was also of use to him in tasks which varied from checking up on the progress of the Clarendon Building in Oxford which he had designed to arranging a consignment of venison from Woodstock Park to Kensington. Joynes became a competent though not inspired architect, but the bath house in the grounds of Carshalton House, of about 1715, which may confidently be attributed to him, seems to look back to the castle ideas of Vanbrugh and Hawksmoor and forward to the engineers' architecture of the nineteenth century.

Ill. 39

Ill. 38

Hawksmoor's correspondence with Joynes covers the years 1705–13, with Joynes's letter of 1715 relating to the prospect of his Kensington appointment and an isolated inquiry of the same year from Hawksmoor about Oxford; letters also survive between Joynes and Vanbrugh. It is quite clear from these documents that Vanbrugh was the chief architect and Hawksmoor his recognized subordinate partner rather than his 'ghost'. In 1722 Hawksmoor described his position as 'like a loving Nurse that almost thinks the Child her own': Blenheim was something less than his 'owne children' like Easton Neston. The plan, the portico, the combination of a large and a small order on the north front, the varied textures, the fantastic skyline, the relationships of massing which change as the spectator moves, the whole dramatic effect, can all be paralleled in Vanbrugh's other buildings. But certain elements of the exterior do not recur in his work after Blenheim: the *amount* of surface detail and the complexity of the detail. By 1707 Vanbrugh was writing of his intention to recase Kimbolton with 'Something of the Castle air', relying on masses and shadows without the use of the orders or any ornaments. Later that year, again concerning Kimbolton, he observed that ''tis certainly the Figure and Proportions that make the most pleasing Fabrick And not the delicacy of the Ornaments'. It is

Ill. 40

40 Vanbrugh. Kimbolton Castle. West front

quite possible that this judgment – of great significance for Vanbrugh's later work – is based as much on knowledge of Hawksmoor's early work as on Vanbrugh's personal reaction to the critical writings of René Rapin and others. The fact is that the exteriors of Castle Howard and Blenheim are not only more ornate than Vanbrugh's other works but more ornate than Hawksmoor's other works; they represent both their remarkable collaboration and a phase of English architecture in which decoration formed a skin over the whole surface of the building. This phase began with the elevations of Wren's St Paul's (which recent cleaning has revealed again) and continued through the Hampton Court scheme and the grander houses of Talman to Easton Neston, Castle Howard and Blenheim. Ultimately it depends on seventeenth-century France. It has for long been recognized that by 1715 Vanbrugh's vocabulary was becoming increasingly oriented towards High Renaissance Italy, but the same is true of Hawksmoor though to a lesser extent. The prodigious nature of Blenheim, its evident costliness (and to the public purse at that), and the further associations of the disgrace of Marlborough in 1711–12, made it the focus of all reaction against the Baroque style in the 1710s. A claim such as John James's in 1711 that 'the Beautys of Architecture may consist with the Greatest plainness of the Structure' carries, in its context of the ruinous expense of building, as direct a reference to Blenheim as Shaftesbury's 'great man' who, in the words of the *Letter concerning design* (1712), 'raises, at a vast expence, such a false and counterfeit Piece of Magnificence, as can be justly arraign'd for its Deformity'. Hawksmoor and Vanbrugh took no part in this reaction. Vanbrugh resigned in 1716 because he found intolerable the behaviour of the Duchess, who disliked him most of all architects. Hawksmoor slipped away, was recalled in 1722 to help her with the interior and environs, but slipped away again in 1725. But neither was ever ashamed of the place. They never tried to repeat its style, firstly because they never again had occasion for close collaboration and

Ill. 13
Ills. 7, 14
Ill. 139

41 Blenheim Palace. Corner tower

secondly because their own styles moved on and away from the Castle Howard-Blenheim style.

Hawksmoor's hand is most securely noticeable in what he called the 'Eminencys', the multitude of towers that make the Blenheim roof-line. They embody a kind of architectural sculpture whose interplay of shapes, of voids and solids, of prismatic and also of convex and concave forms, is only to be found elsewhere in his church steeples and to a lesser extent in some of the Wren steeples and the west towers of St Paul's. Indeed the steeple of Wren's St James, Garlickhythe was not built until 1714–17, and date as well as style suggests that it was to Hawksmoor's design. At Blenheim he probably designed

Ills. 36, 41

Ill. 105

Ill. 42

42 London. St James, Garlickhythe. Steeple

45 Blenheim. East (Hensington) gate ▶

44 Canterbury. Former archbishop's throne

43 Castle Howard. Garden pedestal

both the corner and middle towers of the main block and those over the gateways of the kitchen and stable courts. These structures, like the piers of the Hensington Gate originally in the east garden, the garden pedestals of Castle Howard, or the former archbishop's throne at Canterbury, exemplify a tendency, towards making virtually independent sculptural objects which Hawksmoor was later to take further (p. 191). He also made the drawing for the saloon doorcases of 1712 which employ the Michelangelesque triglyph impost mouldings

Ill. 36
Ill. 45
Ill. 43
Ill. 44
Ills. 168, 172
Ill. 46

47 Early drawing for the hall at Blenheim

46 Blenheim. Saloon doorcase

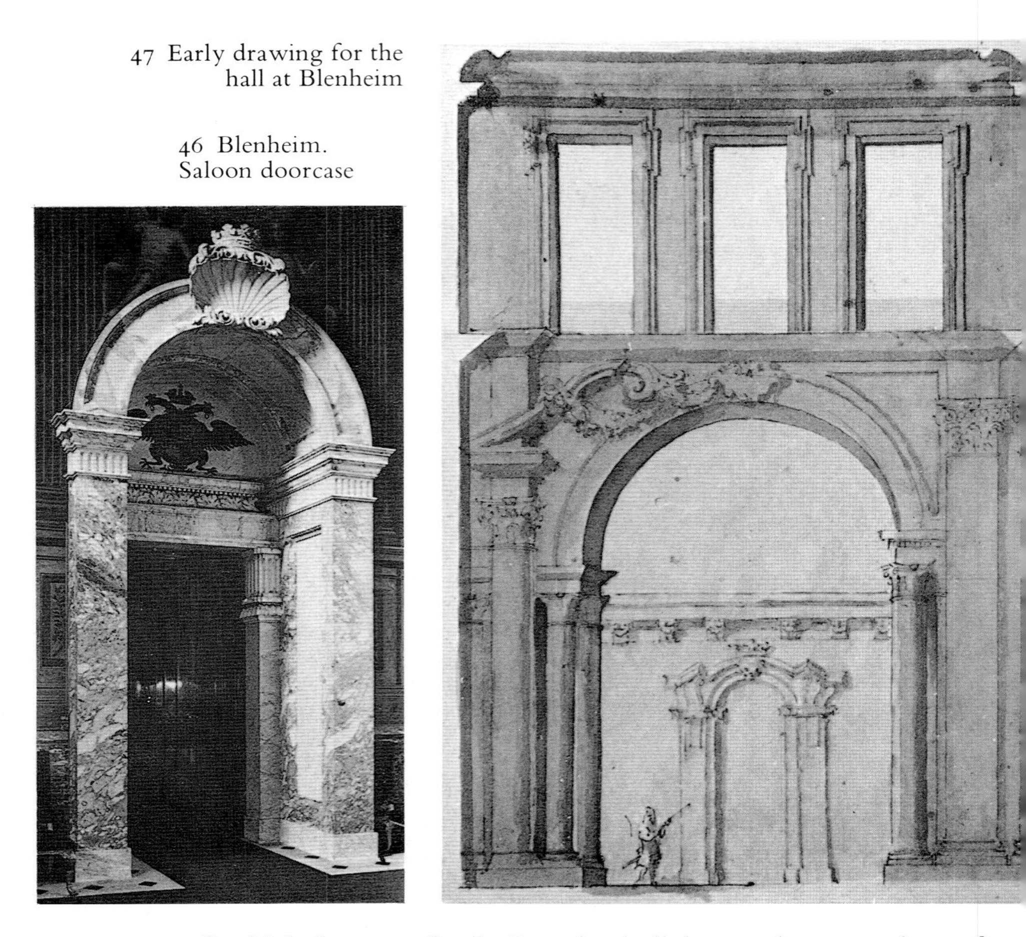

of which he was fond. For the hall he made a number of projects which include both the superimposed arcades and the proscenium arch at the south end framing the door into the saloon. A charming drawing for this shows alternative treatments of a semicircular arch with a standard six-foot man who vividly gives the scale; the doorcase in this drawing refers directly to Borromini. The arcading of the hall is a device which recurs in Vanbrugh's later houses, but with a significantly rougher flavour.

Ill. 48
Ill. 47

Little of the interior beyond the hall dates from the first period of Blenheim. From October 1710, when the Duchess stopped the work until the Treasury should send money to pay the workmen's arrears, the building suffered a six years' succession of crises, culminating in Vanbrugh's resignation. At the end of 1716 Thornhill put the last touches to the hall ceiling and the Duchess enlisted a cabinet-maker named Moore as her 'oracle' on matters of building. In 1719 she and the Duke moved into the eastern part of the house and

48 Blenheim. The hall

Marlborough died (at Windsor) three years later. His widow's completion of Blenheim – conclusion is perhaps a better word – with Hawksmoor's help belongs to a later chapter (p. 182).

A minor but impressive royal building erected at the time Blenheim was being planned (1704–5) must be Hawksmoor's work although there is no more than stylistic evidence: the brick Orangery or greenhouse at Kensington Palace. Vanbrugh, as Comptroller, discovered that the bricklayers were in the employ of Benjamin Jackson, the Queen's Master Mason, and altered the 'draft'; there is, however, no implication in Vanbrugh's letter of November 1704 to Godolphin that he was the designer. The patterning of round-headed windows and pediments in the centre and end frontispieces and the niche-like recesses in the attic ends link the front of the Orangery with the north front of Easton Neston and with the eminencies of Blenheim. Inside, the choice and the delicate deployment of mouldings in the circular end rooms, and the spatial contrast between them and the long central hall, reveal a direct descent from the gallery decoration and the spatial complexity of Easton Neston. Moreover, Hawksmoor was Clerk of Works at Kensington until 1715.

Ills. 20, 23

49 Kensington Palace. The Orangery

50 Kensington Palace. The Orangery. Interior

51 Kensington Charity School (destroyed)

From the number of letters to Joynes written from Kensington Hawksmoor's official quarters as Clerk must have been his home during that period. As a resident, he was also a Trustee of Kensington Charity School and designed its new building. This brick structure, built in 1711–12, later became the National School, and was demolished about 1875. It was three bays wide by five deep and had separate boys' and girls' schoolrooms on the upper floors. The tower-like centre of its façade, rising between the vestigial corners of a triangular pediment, anticipated Hawksmoor's solution to the problem of combining tower and church-front at St George-in-the-East.

Ill. 51

Ill. 104

Hawksmoor's engagement at Greenwich is the most likely occasion of his meeting Dr George Clarke, Fellow of All Souls, Oxford from 1680 and joint secretary to the Admiralty 1702–5. Clarke was Hawksmoor's exact contemporary and an amateur architect. The remarkable collection of architectural drawings which he left to Worcester College after quarrelling with his own college includes many by Inigo Jones and Webb which came from Webb's descendants and many by Hawksmoor and other contemporaries; there is nevertheless evidence that some drawings were added or repurchased early in the nineteenth century. Clarke himself designed Christ Church Library and parts of both the Queen's and Worcester Colleges; the last two were the result of collaboration with the Oxford mason William Townesend and advice from Hawksmoor. Clarke was concerned with practically every Oxford building scheme between 1703 and his death in 1736. While it is unlikely that Hawksmoor depended in any way on such a relationship, Clarke seems to have taken the place occupied first by Wren and then by Vanbrugh. As an amateur with ideas he must have revered Hawksmoor's learning and experience; in return the professional attempted, through his intermediacy, to engage Oxford interest in many grand designs. That Hawksmoor did not have more success was not Clarke's fault but that of the senior common rooms of the time and the college benefactors who belonged to them or were connected with them. Benefactors liked to see their money used, but it was difficult to interest either them or dons in the sort of larger comprehensive scheme that would have required more than one donation. Half of All Souls was rebuilt to Hawksmoor's designs, but even that was done piecemeal, section after section; so was Clarke and Townesend's front quadrangle of the Queen's College. The inadequacy of funds was often accompanied by the disposition of college committees to leave things to happen of their own accord – or do nothing. Although Sir Nathaniel Lloyd of All Souls was a particularly volatile benefactor his complaint about Hawksmoor in 1734 is not untypical of the situation: 'The Printed Draughts must bee Altered, and wt Alterations He may think Necessary to make will not bee Easily foreseen – He Designs Grandly, for a College. I will not lead the College and myself into these Difficultys: into new plans, & new Worke, Wee shall not know where it will End.' And a few months after the architect's death he wrote: 'I reckon now, Hawksmooring, and Townsending, is all Out for this Century.'

That Hawksmoor ever got a foot successfully into Oxford architecture was probably due to Clarke's advocacy, to the fact that the prime amateur architect Henry Aldrich, Dean of Christ Church (who probably designed the library of the Queen's College), died in 1710, and to the geographical closeness of Blenheim. His first success was the commission for the Clarendon Press building at the end of Broad Street, built 1712–13. The Clarke collection contains drawings by several hands, from which it appears as if certain features, the central Doric engaged or full portico and the disposition of the plan either side of a central corridor (to accommodate the Bible press and the learned book press), were stipulated by the University. Hawksmoor's letters show that the construction

Ills. 52, 53

52 Oxford. Old Clarendon Building. South front

53 Oxford. Old Clarendon Building. North front

was in his care; autograph drawings confirm that he designed it. Besides those for the final design there are several alternatives. The central corridor allows the building to act as a triumphal arch between the street and the Schools Quadrangle on the south, and one drawing offers a solution even more heroic in scale than the final one. In this the usual disposition of such a façade is reversed so that the centre portico has a flat roof and

Ill. 54

54 Early design for the Clarendon Building

the pediment is enlarged to form a gigantic gable spanning the whole width of the building. The effect from the side would have been like the portico to a giant but non-existent building, and the other designs are more orthodox though still powerful. In the final one the wall surface is cut back in layers, a device invented by Michelangelo which explores the depth of the masonry and takes over from the windows and pillars the definition and regulation of the façade. The language of the Writing School, of mass, weight and severity, has become enriched and refined. It stands as the one executed portion of Hawksmoor's heroic vision for Oxford, a vision which the Gothick magic of All Souls does not approach in grandeur and which is only partly reflected in the work of Clarke and Townesend.

Ill. 55

55 George Clarke and William Townesend. Oxford. The Queen's College

Hawksmoor's concern with Oxford dates back to 1708–9; at this time projects for the 'Printing House' were already being considered, and the Vice-Chancellor of the University was at that time William Lancaster, Provost of the Queen's College. The foundation stone of that college's new buildings was laid on 6 February 1710, and Hawksmoor's proposals, which were not carried out, can be dated 1708–9 on internal evidence. With characteristic liberality of invention he sent at least seven alternative plans and sets of elevations for two of them. At the same date he was among the designers from whom Clarke obtained projects for new buildings for All Souls. In the drawings for the two colleges, near but not adjoining neighbours on the north side of the High Street, certain ideas were common or transferable, and one sheet of paper was used

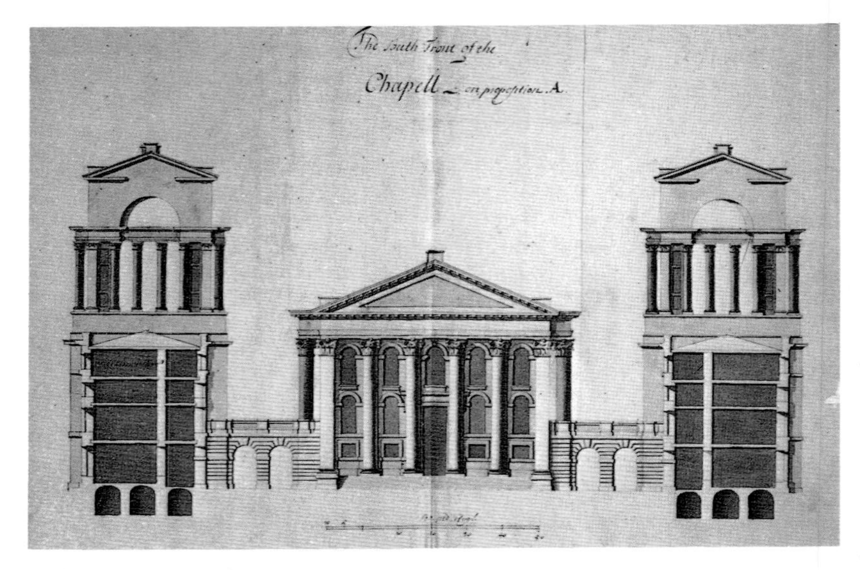

56 Proposition A for the Queen's College. Chapel front

for both buildings in turn. Within the period of about a year, however, no order of priority can be established for the various schemes.

The Queen's College schemes are for a completely new complex except for the north range at the back (which had just been finished in 1707) and the library of 1692–4 on the north-west. Hawksmoor suggested several variations on the theme of two courts, one behind the other, separated by a range of building. The plan numbered IV, for which there are elevations, has a gigantic screen on the street front between end blocks which contain living rooms; the central feature, with its sixty-foot columns and (drawn in pencil and erased) the suggestion of a statue of a female figure, perhaps the Queen, could only make sense as a kind of steeple to be seen obliquely *Ill. 57* as one approached along the street. In this design the hall and chapel are placed (as in the building) between the two quad-

57 Proposition IV for the Queen's College. Street front

rangles; this arrangement may have been reintroduced to Oxford by Hawksmoor from Wren's planning of Chelsea Hospital, but Oxford had offered Wren a precedent in his old college, the Jacobean Wadham.

The other plan with elevations, marked A, shows the hall and kitchen on the street front, either side of the entrance, and a free-standing chapel between the quadrangles. This remarkable building, more orthodox than the Clarendon design, is fronted by a giant hexastyle temple portico and entered on the short axis; the shape of the interior implies that the altar is then to the spectator's right. The change of direction anticipates the similar one in St George, Bloomsbury (p. 132) which also has a hexastyle portico. There are also connections with Blenheim: the three ranges of windows like those which light the hall of Blenheim behind its portico, and the shallow broad attic structures at the extremities which are of the same

Ill. 56

Ill. 58

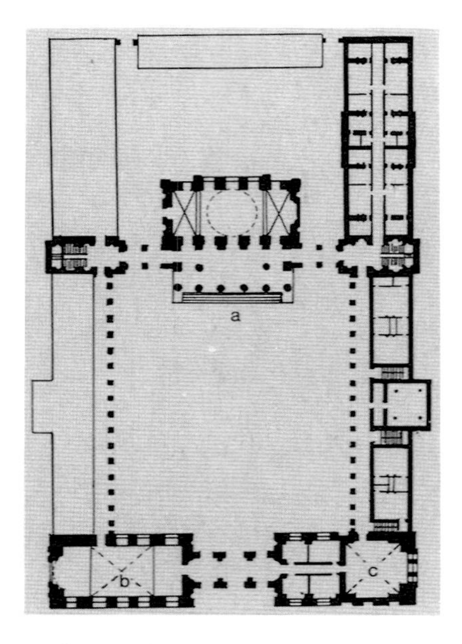

58 Proposition A for the Queen's College. Plan: (a) chapel, (b) hall, (c) kitchen

59 Oval chapel project for the Queen's College

order as the roof lanterns of Blenheim. There appears thus to be some genetic evidence for the similarity of feeling between the Blenheim hall and the inside of the Bloomsbury church and the college design. Hawksmoor also considered an oval plan at one stage both for Bloomsbury and the Queen's chapel. *Ill. 59*

The plan of the north-east range in project A contains one innovation which runs counter to college planning of its date and considerably later: a central corridor. In large houses of the seventeenth century, which were planned and inhabited in horizontal layers, the corridor (p. 48) increased the privacy of rooms by giving them each direct access to the entrance or the staircase. Wren evolved corridors in the ward-blocks of Chelsea and Greenwich by a process of division in which the individual cubicles of the pensioners were partly screened and partly curtained off from an access corridor; these buildings again were used horizontally. College planning, which had for long allowed scholars a combination of privacy with close proximity, was based on the vertical principle of the *staircase*, in

which accessible neighbours are either across the landing or on the floor above or below. Hawksmoor's plan therefore breaks completely with tradition, and it is not surprising that it made no mark whatever in Oxford. It is, however, interesting that in the corners of Easton Neston he had adopted the staircase principle. *Ill. 21*

The history of the All Souls rebuilding schemes begins in 1703 when Dr Clarke proposed to build a house for his own use, to revert to the College on his death. A site was suggested in the cloister at the north (back) end of the college, and most of the cloister was rather hastily demolished. The project was then resited at the front, and Clarke's ideas expanded into schemes for new lodging blocks on two sites. One was on the north, partly on the cloister site and partly on land acquired for the purpose by exchange with New College; the other site, on the High Street front, would have entailed demolition of the medieval street front. At first (1708–9) these sites were probably alternatives, and it was probably the death of Christopher Codrington in 1710 and news of his bequest of books and money for a new library that suggested to Clarke and Hawksmoor the prospect of building on both sites and in effect rebuilding completely except for the chapel. The building by Hawksmoor of the library on the north side and the rest of the north quadrangle was the final outcome of these projects, but the work was not begun until 1716 and belongs to a later section (p. 163). Drawings were made at various dates before this, but most of the ideas go back to the projects of 1708–9 for a block 200 feet long, embodying similar themes and equal grandeur to the Queen's College schemes.

As with the Clarendon Building, the drawings by various hands in the Clarke collection for the north lodgings project have common features that imply a specific brief: in this case a central portico in front of a common room, with lodgings to each side. Hawksmoor's elevations are based on the same formula as Webb's King Charles Block: a giant order, a central portico with a pediment, and secondary emphasis in the end bays. The problems of coherence and vertical emphasis in a long elevation were attacked in various ways. One elevation is divided into a few large units with huge end bays of a scale unexpected in proportion to the building and with little relation to the uniform sets of rooms within. The portico, like that in the early Clarendon Building design, is dramatized; here the

Ill. 5

Ill. 60

Ill. 54

60 Project for north lodging at All Souls

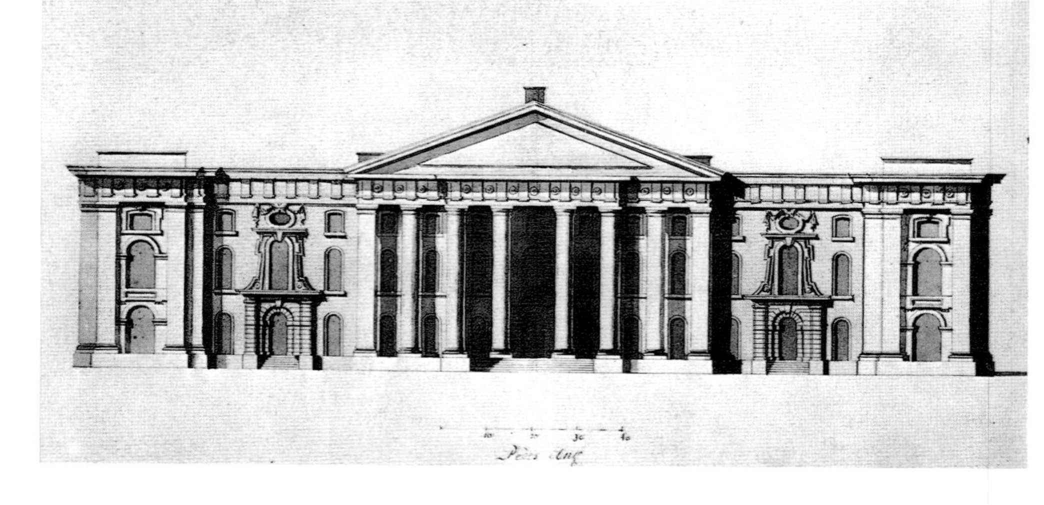

61 Alternative project for All Souls

recess is only three bays wide but the portico and pediment are extended to seven bays. The intermediate entrances confirm that the interior was to be arranged by staircases, but one at least of the other elevations, which all have some sort of attic feature for central emphasis, is related to a plan with corridors giving access to sets of rooms. The placing of the corridors, the portico and the great room behind it suggests that here Blenheim rather than Wren's ward-blocks was in Hawksmoor's mind.

Ills. 61, 62

Ill. 160

62 Plan of Ill. 61

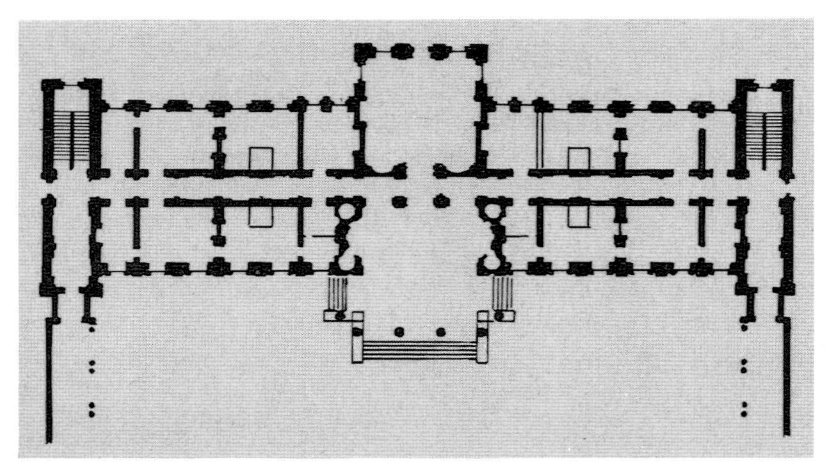

63 Detail of a project for All Souls

64 Noorwits and Van Bassen. The Hague. Nieuwe Kerk. Porch

In the street elevation projects the central gate takes the place of the portico. In the 'classical' version a Doric triumphal arch carries an attic surmounted by an arched structure which is drawn in perspective like the domed peristyle of twenty columns which in turn it supports. The urns on some of the All Souls elevations are quite clearly drawn not as ordinary containers but as giant banded eggs, symbolizing the breaking of the bonds of death at the Last Judgment. The most spectacular examples of this are the stone eggs over the porch of the Nieuwe Kerk in the Hague, but the symbolism is particularly appropriate to the college of All Souls. It is thus probable that the peristyle is not merely a formal descendant of Bramante's Tempietto or the domes of St Paul's and Greenwich, nor merely an example of Hawksmoor's liking for placing autonomous architectural forms on pedestals, but also another stage in the sequence of circular memorial or funerary buildings which for him culminated in the Mausoleum (p. 198). The second elevation is, like the designs for Warwick, an experiment in Gothick. Hawksmoor did not distinguish clearly between Gothic and Romanesque, and the reliance on mass rather than line is as un-Gothic as the round-headed windows which derive directly from Hugh May's medievalizing exteriors at Windsor Castle. But the clue to this drawing is in

Ill. 65

Ill. 63

Ill. 64

Ill. 15

Ill. 66

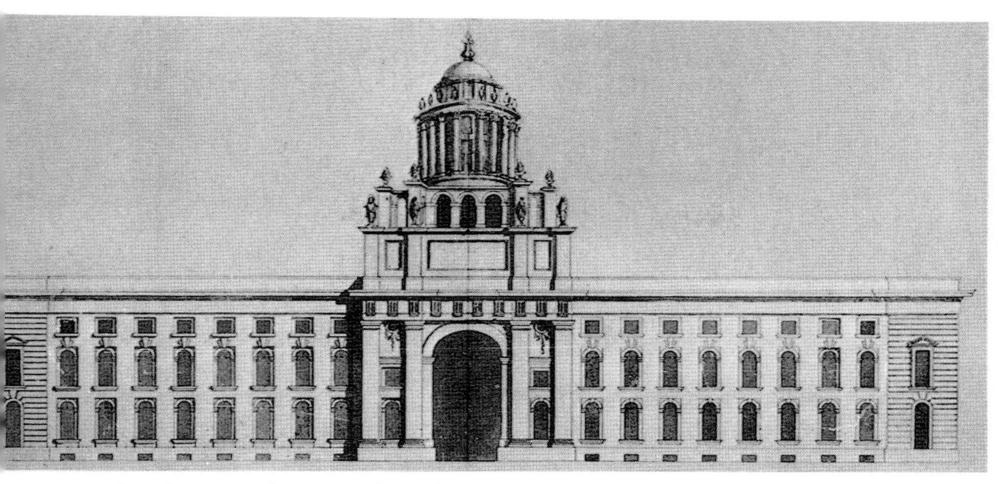

65 Project for street front at All Souls

66 Project for Gothick street front at All Souls

the monstrous pinnacles, the deep shaded arch whose tympanum carries an unidentifiable relief, and the barely disguised triangular pediment above it. The medieval details are incidental to the basic styleless forms of the building, and Hawksmoor seems here for the first time to be offering consciously alternative, almost interchangeable, styles. Before building finally began he was to make the options explicit.

Ill. 177

The conformity with the medieval work that was finally chosen at All Souls was not the only kind of relationship Hawksmoor could imagine. In his designs for King's College, Cambridge (1712–13) he took disparity of elevation not only to the point where it seems to be a principle but even to the point of stylistic disintegration. When Dr John Adams became Provost in 1712 he determined to press forward the completion of the college founded by Henry VI. Through Wren he met Hawksmoor, who offered a set of plans and elevations for a whole college, larger than any of the Oxford projects, roughly following the founder's specification and incorporating as its chief jewel the old chapel, 300 feet long and 130 feet to the top of the corner turrets. The problem was thus partly one of scale, and while the east and west ranges of the court have lodging blocks with three-storey elevations the court side of the south range, containing the hall and kitchen, has a truly giant Doric arcade which half conceals two tiers of windows and offers some parity of scale with the great windows and buttresses of the chapel on the north. The second court,

Ills. 67, 68

67 Project for King's College, Cambridge. Reconstruction, looking north-west

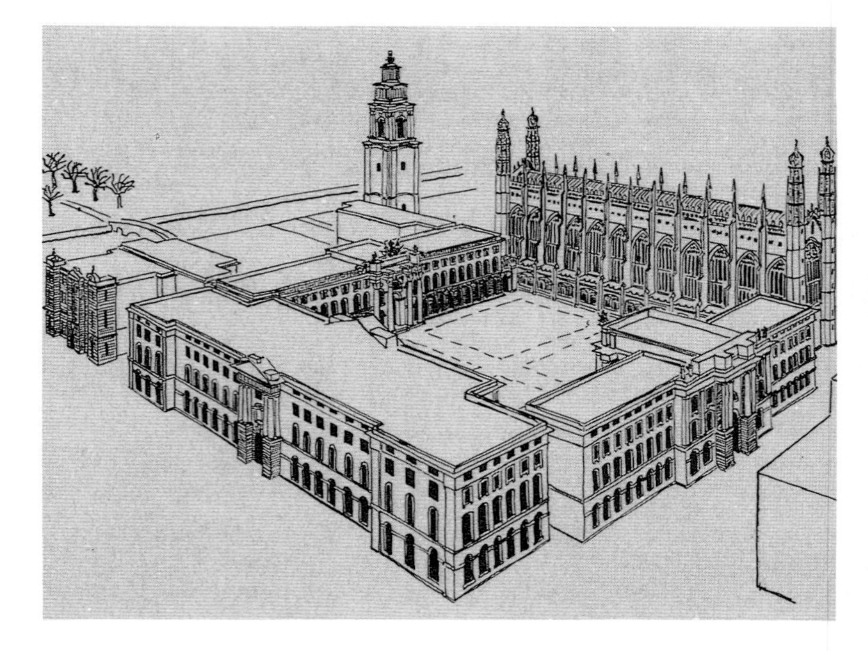

68 Project for King's College, Cambridge. Reconstruction, looking south-west

towards the river, is known in less detail; the outer face of the southern building, intended for the Provost's lodging, is in a totally different vocabulary drawn from the heavy rustication, dropped keystones, giant masks and unexpected pediments of Italian or even northern Mannerism. North of the *Ill. 69*

69 Design for the Provost's house at King's College

70 Design for a campanile at King's College

court is a precinct containing a big bell-tower, a feature intended by Henry VI although not in Hawksmoor's form with its Borrominesque concave walls and concave-convex lantern. *Ill. 70*

In response to Adams's wish to have the chapel front unobscured by the lodging ranges, Hawksmoor produced a revised plan with a wider court after March 1713. Two wooden models were also made for the western range; one relates directly to the revised scheme. *Ill. 71* In both models Hawksmoor arranged for partly shared accommodation: each chamber was to have two occupants but each occupant was to have his own study and bedroom, one at chamber level and the other up on a mezzanine reached by a private staircase. In the first model this

71 Model for Fellows' Building at King's College

arrangement is not apparent outside, but in the second the river front has, like parts of Easton Neston, twice as many tiers of windows as the rest.

Adams's death in 1719 meant the end of his personal commitment, which had included the energetic raising of a building fund. It meant in consequence the end of Hawksmoor's design. In 1722 James Gibbs was approached, and in 1724 the west range that bears his name today was begun; the great lunettes in the centre of his elevations are perhaps an echo of Hawksmoor's model. The great scheme had no other practical effect, but drawings now to be considered show that in Hawksmoor's own mind it was the starting point for one even grander and more far-reaching.

72 'Third' project for Greenwich Hospital. Chapel elevation

CHAPTER FOUR

Exploration

In 1711 Hawksmoor was fifty. He had already suffered the first attacks of 'gout', a name that is probably generic for the ailments that were in various later periods to confine him to bed, to make him for weeks on end unable to write or draw, and finally as 'gout in the stomach' to kill him. The Obituary tells us that its most poignant pains could never ruffle or discompose his temper, a hyperbole which must mean at least that he recognized that he had to live with it. But the future of architecture still seemed to be in his and Vanbrugh's hands, and in those of Thomas Archer and James Gibbs who had first-hand knowledge of European Baroque architecture. Wren at 79 still presided – officially – over the Office of Works. St Paul's Cathedral was finished. Greenwich, Castle Howard and Blenheim were in the doldrums but, as all great building works proceeded by fits and starts according to the weather and the supply of money, the situation was not yet one to arouse anxiety in addition to impatience. At Oxford Hawksmoor had lost the Queen's College commission but had hopes of All Souls and the Clarendon Building. The collapse in a storm in November 1710 of the old church of Greenwich started a train of events which led to the Fifty New Churches Act of 1711 and his appointment that October as one of the two surveyors to the Commission it established (p. 104).

It may be an accident that we have a whole group of environmental plans dating between 1711 and 1713; on the other hand the concentration of these schemes within a short period may be the result of an increased interest on his part and a certain amount of leisure between the run-down of the works on which he had earlier been engaged and the intensive construction of several churches in the period beginning in 1714. It should not, however, be imagined that at no other time was he interested in environmental schemes: at Greenwich he seems to have begun much earlier and continued until at least 1728, and in 1735–6 he was planning an arcaded Parliament Street, 110 feet wide, as the approach to the projected Westminster Bridge for which he also made a design.

Even at Greenwich, however, the earliest *dated* drawings belong to 1711, when Hawksmoor probably took out for neither the first nor the last time a folder of sketches for the enlargement of the Hospital. The completion of St Paul's gave the Greenwich directors incentive and pretext to petition Parliament for financial help in April 1711. The Fifty New Churches Act, itself framed and carried partly on the release of the coal tax out of which St Paul's was financed, included an allocation for Greenwich that may have been the immediate spur for Hawksmoor's 1711 scheme. The project for a 'piazza' round St Paul's, often attributed to Wren but drawn by Hawksmoor, is most likely to have been conceived on the completion of the cathedral. Concern with the new churches also led Hawksmoor to consider environment in at least one case, in the plan for a 'Basilica after the Primitive Christians'. The shift of activity at Castle Howard from the house to the gardens about 1712 may also have engaged his interest if not his activity, and finally that year saw him planning new urban centres for Oxford and Cambridge to incorporate his university designs.

Ill. 73

Ill. 87

Because, of all the fine arts, architecture is the one most nearly tied to utility, it is natural to feel that unrealized schemes are not properly architecture. Drawings of extraordinary vision are not sufficient in themselves, as the drawings of a painter may often be. The situation is made more difficult by the fact that many architects' drawings are not in themselves either attractive to the layman or intelligible to him without more interpretation than he would believe himself to need for painters' drawings. But drawings not only play a vital part in the documentation of Hawksmoor's development and achievement; they also tell us all we know about those visionary schemes which far exceeded the material opportunities at his disposal. Nevertheless, once this is admitted and the danger of diminishing his stature by omission is obviated, it is possible to incur an equally serious risk of misinterpretation. All the world loves the figure who tries hard and falls short, and this figure is easily and romantically distorted into the pawn of fate, the victim of circumstances, the prophet not honoured in his own country (or any other), the genius whom nobody understood. Hawksmoor did not have an easy life, and in 1721 Vanbrugh was shamed into writing that the French would have known how to use him far better than the 'Barbarous Age' into which 'his fine, ingenious Parts' had fallen. But the Vitruvian tripos of Commodity, Firmness and Delight recognizes the fact that architects are the most practical and also the most unpractical of men. The Palladian amateur Sir Thomas Robinson conceded that he had 'never talk'd with a more reasonable man, nor with one so little prejudiced in favour of his own performances'. The Duchess of Marlborough thought him honest, modest and economical (she thought Vanbrugh none of these things) and recorded the help he had given Godolphin in 'lights how to reform many abuses in the queens works'. This was the common-sense Hawksmoor, the teacher of Henry Joynes, the careful aide of Vanbrugh, the man concerned with fire precautions, the man people on occasion forgot to pay. Yet Hawksmoor at the drawing-board was the man who saw, in the £48,000 voted by Parliament to complete Greenwich – a sum enough for little beyond a decent structure – renewed hope for schemes that would have rivalled Versailles and St Peter's in grandeur. Here was the man who, asked for a design, would offer six; whose effects in the 1740 sale included twenty-eight drawings by him to illustrate that enormous, improbable and unknowable monument of Antiquity, the Tomb of Porsenna. This book is principally concerned with those of his designs that came to fruition; none-theless it may not be inappropriate that the middle chapter should be an attempt to *realize*, as a harpsichordist does a figured bass, those designs which could never be constructed. Never, at least in the absence of a ruler with absolute power and infinite material resources, such as the Baroque popes and Louis XIV had been and the English monarchs could or would not be, or were not allowed to be. Hawksmoor had nothing good to say for the way London was rebuilt after the Great Fire – there is a vehement passage in a letter to Clarke of 1715 – and the *Remarks* on Greenwich Hospital (1728) seems to be the starting point of the legend, given wider currency by the Wren *Parentalia* (1750), that Wren's rapidly conceived plan for the city was accepted by King and Parliament but defeated by the self-interest of the citizens.

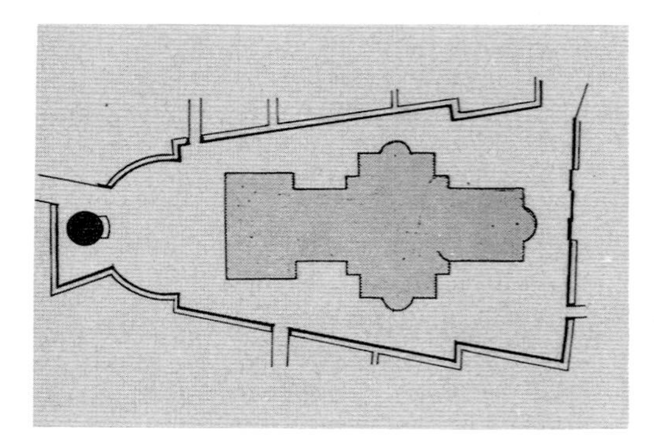

73 Project for St Paul's 'piazza'

74 Project for St Paul's baptistery

The scheme for St Paul's Churchyard, which probably dates from the completion of the Cathedral in 1710, is for a wedge-shaped precinct more or less generally symmetrical with the church and partly, but not entirely, based on the existing streets and open spaces. Though the plans and elevations are in Hawksmoor's hand Wren's participation cannot be ruled out, but the building at the west end usually called a baptistery is certainly Hawksmoor's design. This would have equalled the body of the church in height; the five-storey buildings with ground-floor arcades which lined the entire

Ill. 73

Ill. 74

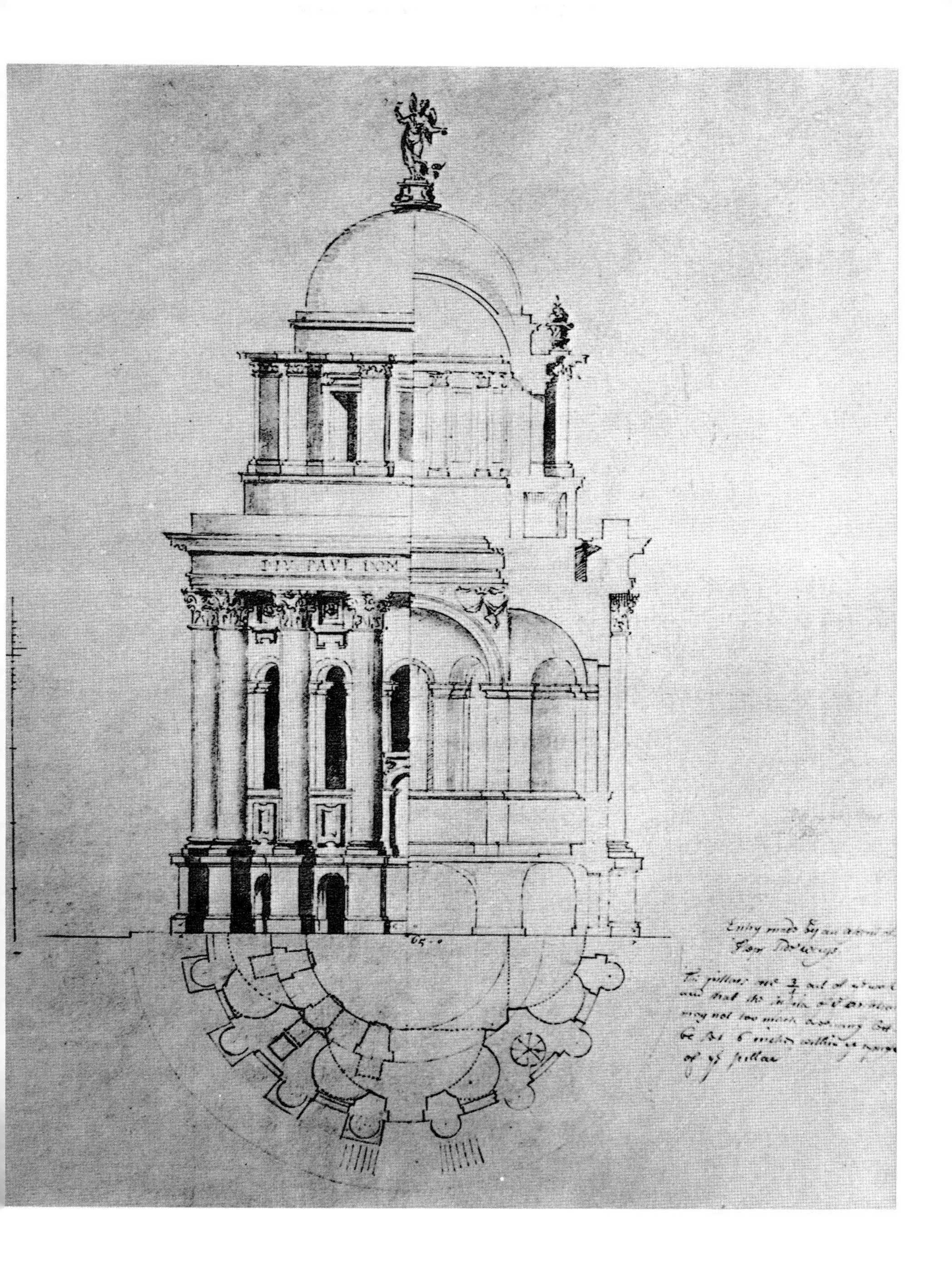
DIV PAVL DOM

area, broken only by streets and alleys, would only have been about fifty feet or the height of the lower storey of the church elevation. Present-day arguments about the setting of St Paul's sometimes overlook the fact that no buildings of its time were higher than this, except steeples. St Paul's would have dominated the piazza, as it dominated the city, but the piazza like the city was irregular. Its main axis did not coincide with that of the church, and the approach streets would have offered interesting but not symmetrical views of the building.

The plan of 1712 of 'the town of Cambridge as it now ought to be reformed' was also based on an existing irregular urban centre; Hawksmoor probably began with the axially planned King's College scheme (p. 80) but he retained the town's Y-shaped street plan, making comparatively minor widenings and realignments and co-ordinating buildings and vistas. Besides the new college he planned a 'Forum' east of it, with a building in two halves facing it and comprising a university church and a 'Commencement Hall' for academic ceremonies. A vista through the Forum was to link the chapel and the new bell-tower with the gate of Christ's College far to the east. North of the Forum, partly closed at each end, the street past St John's College was to become a kind of Roman circus like the Piazza Navona. The two objects near its ends are probably obelisks; this probably approaches certainty in view of the precedent stated on the plan: 'It wou'd be very impertinent in me, to desire so much good and, I humbly Ask pardon for Making such a plan, and hope I may be excused because Cavalier Fontana and others has done ye same in Case of Like Nature.' There is other evidence that for Hawksmoor the Cavaliere Fontana meant not Carlo (1634–1714), master of Gibbs in Rome and the Italian selected after Bernini and Borromini for censure by Colin Campbell, but Domenico (1543–1607), architect to Pope Sixtus V in the resiting of the Vatican obelisk and the replanning of Rome by means of a network of straight streets aligned on existing or specially provided monuments. Hawksmoor saw Fontana as the obelisk

Ill. 75

75 Plan for Cambridge

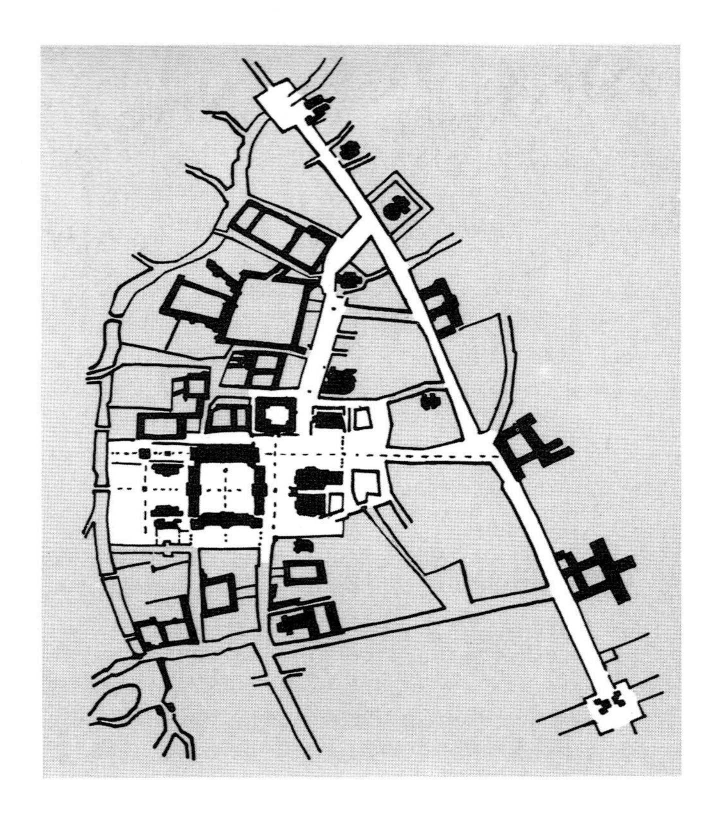

and vista man; his conception of Sixtine Rome must have derived from the pages of Fontana's book on the Vatican obelisk and from engraved views. In the Cambridge plan he attached himself firmly to the archetype of Baroque town planning.

One of the Oxford plans is dated August 1713 and the other two may not be much earlier. Whereas the Cambridge plan is constructed round one project, King's College, at Oxford several existing or proposed buildings had to be incorporated; the predominance in the Oxford plans of solid things, buildings, over vistas, may therefore be due to a more complex situation rather than to any change in Hawksmoor's ideas. While the Cambridge plan was based on an accurate enlargement of Loggan's 1688 engraved map, the Oxford

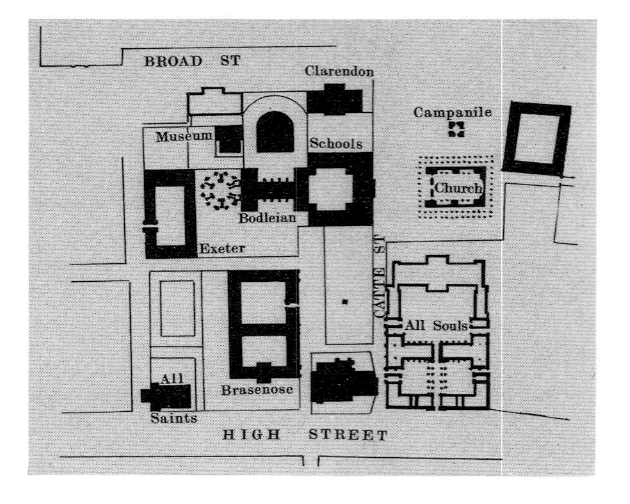

76 Plan for Oxford

77 'Regio prima' at Oxford

plans were based on inaccurate drawn surveys (which are also extant) and presuppose more space in some places than was really available.

The plans are for the area north of the High Street on either side of St Mary's Church, including a rebuilt All Souls, a regularized Brasenose College, a building on the north more or less as a pendant to the Clarendon Press on the far side of the Sheldonian Theatre, and a large new university church north of All Souls on the site of Hart Hall (now Hertford College). One plan is altogether more ambitious in scope, for it extends as far west as a *Forum Civitatis* at Carfax, a colonnaded square with a spiral column like Trajan's, and far enough east to include the Queen's College and the old wall enclosing New College Garden. There were to be two big and two smaller gateways, and New College Garden could be entered through the Mound by a 'Pausilyp', a term coined by Hawksmoor for an underground road by derivation from the tunnel of Posillipo near Naples. This plan implies that his ideas went even further, for it is entitled *Regio Prima* as if there should be a further development south of the High Street.

Ill. 76

Ill. 77

The church is on the plan of a peripteral temple, but since in one drawing it is fourteen columns by twelve and has some sort of side chapels Hawksmoor may have thought of a cleres-

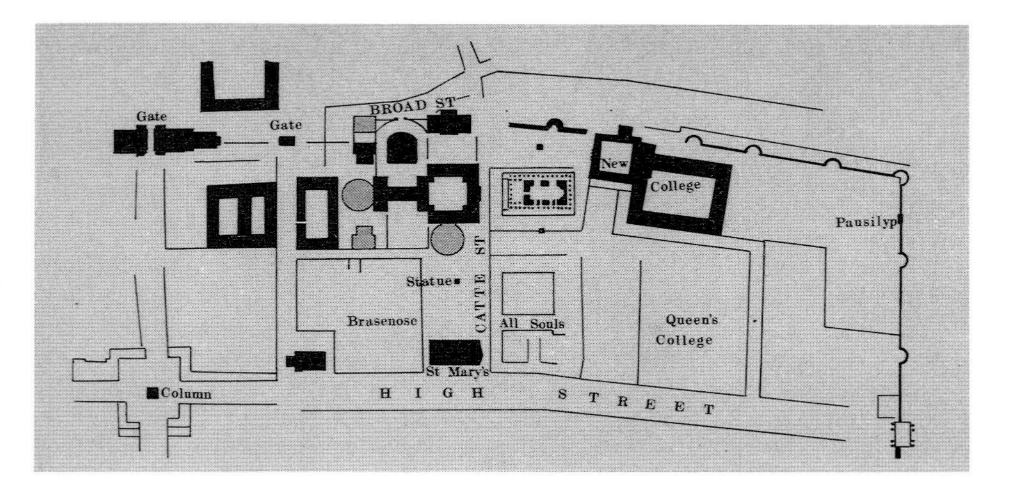

tory rising through and above the peristyle to light the interior. This device would also have reduced the pediment from a span of twelve columns to eight. Even so, it would have been grander than Gibbs's church designs or other experiments of the 1710s on the themes of the peripteral temple and the temple-front portico (p. 137).

The three Oxford plans show one other building that was to affect very strongly and visibly the future of the area: the Radcliffe Library. Between them they show it on two different sites: attached to the west end of the old Bodleian and to the south side of the Schools quadrangle facing St Mary's Church. The latter site entailed the demolition of the small houses on Catte Street opposite All Souls and the opening up of the area to make Radcliffe Square.

Dr John Radcliffe had decided by 1712 to adorn the University and perpetuate his own memory by paying part of the cost of a new library building added to the west end of the Bodleian. Two years later he had changed the site to the south of the Schools quadrangle. Between 1712 and 1715 Hawksmoor made at least seven different designs; at this stage his activity was probably directed once more to Clarke and entirely unofficial and speculative, and in April 1715 he was inquiring of Joynes what the University intended to do. In 1720, having

78 Model for the Radcliffe Library

bought and demolished some houses, Radcliffe's Trustees decided to approach all the leading figures in English Baroque architecture – their Minutes name them, including Hawksmoor; nothing was done until the construction of a wooden model to a new design of his in 1733–4. The conception of the circular domed building ringed with columns, present in several of the designs and the later model, was taken over by Gibbs in the executed building; Gibbs's outstanding contribution was to sever the library from the Schools and place it in the centre of Radcliffe Square. But both the germ of the building and the idea of the square were Hawksmoor's.

Ills. 78, 79

The difference already shown between the Cambridge and the Oxford plans, that in the latter the main axes are the centre lines of buildings and not of open spaces, resulted in a more 'free' sort of planning for Oxford. The axes could only be seen on paper; thus it would not be possible to perceive directly the order underlying an often apparently random placing of buildings. It is obviously impossible to experience fully from drawings the spatial effect of either the random appearance or the underlying order. However, the surprise of finding Gibbs's great rotunda as one enters the square from either end of Catte Street today is as much Hawksmoor's work as Gibbs's.

Ill. 80

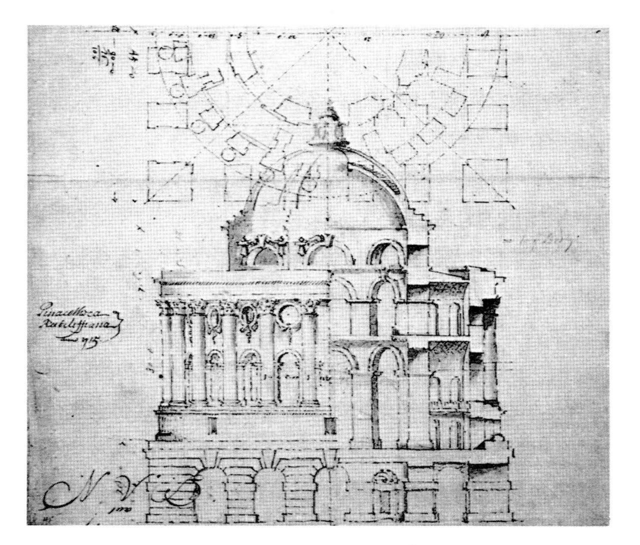

79 Project for the Radcliffe Library

80 James Gibbs. Oxford. The Radcliffe Camera

82 'Second' plan for Greenwich Hospital. (a) Observatory, (b) Grotto, (c) Queen's House, (d) Chapel, (e) 'Pausilippo', (f) River Thames

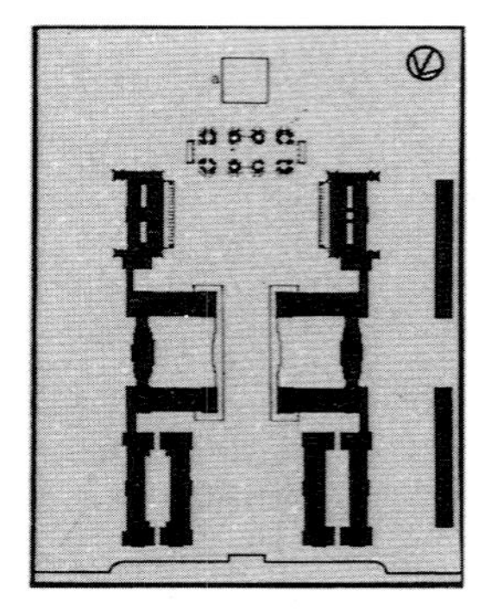

81 'First' plan for Greenwich Hospital. (a) Queen's House

Ill. 28

With Greenwich we have at least enough in the way of buildings and setting to appreciate the basic problem and how much we miss through the fact that Hawksmoor was never allowed to solve it. The Queen's House is too insignificant for the vista between Wren's twin masses of domes and colonnades; Hawksmoor turned the problem round by considering the latter not as a drama without a proper conclusion but as an overture without a drama. As early as January 1699 three wooden models were made, of the Hospital itself, of the Infirmary, and of the Infirmary with the Church and the Queen's House. The first is probably the model in the National Maritime Museum of the four blocks standing today though not as they were built; the other two, which are lost, offer the earliest evidence of altogether larger ideas for the Hospital – but no evidence of whose ideas they were. Hawksmoor's involvement with Greenwich has been described (p. 43) and most of the drawings for amplification are in his hand. His three schemes, which probably spring from the 1699 models but date from 1705 onwards, all consist of the addition of a further court south of the colonnades, with a big central chapel closing the vista and cutting off the Queen's House. In what may be the earliest scheme the court is rectangular and is flanked by complex wings with colonnades two columns thick; the chapel is a long rectangle of eight quartered piers, carrying vaults and a central dome on pendentives.

Ill. 81

Ill. 83

In a variant of this scheme Hawksmoor suggested putting a chapel beyond the Queen's House up the hill so as to leave the vista open; in the second of his undated schemes he considered moving the house up the hill, continuing the symmetry through the gardens and the exedra or 'grotto' planned by John Webb, and conveniently bringing the Observatory at the top of the hill into line with the axis of everything else. This is the most ambitious scheme of all, with an oval court and a cruciform domed chapel with an eastern apse and porticoes on the other three sides. The oval court and the grouping of dome and bell turrets above it refer directly to St Peter's and its piazza; the width of the latter is a little under twice that of the Greenwich court. The greater extent of this scheme made absolutely necessary the demolition or removal of the Queen's House – and the rearrangement of the old Woolwich road that ran

Ill. 82

Ill. 85

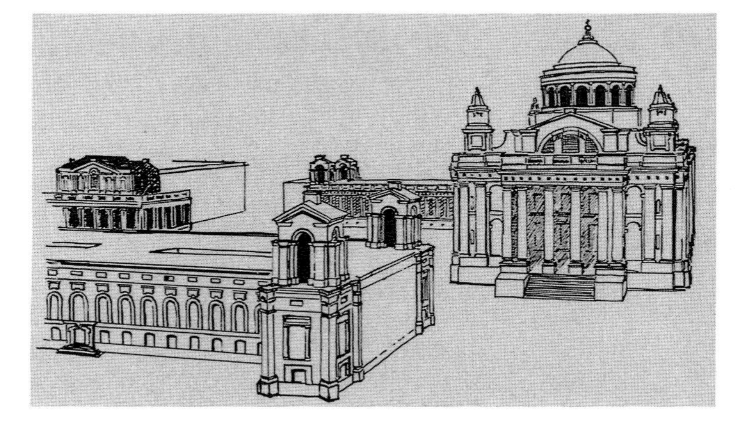

83 'First' project for Greenwich Hospital. Reconstruction from south-west

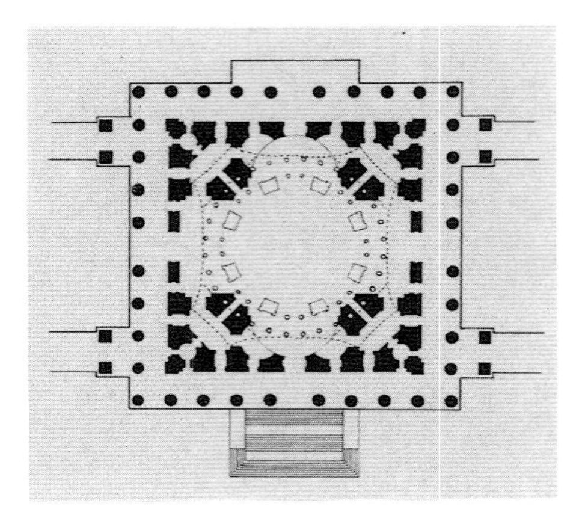

84 'Third' project for Greenwich Hospital. Plan of chapel

86 'Third' project for Greenwich Hospital. Reconstruction from north

through it. Hawksmoor marked on his plan a 'Pausilippo' (p. 92), to take the road underground in a manner disproportionately grand for the country lane it really was. (In fact it had been closed by 1699 when the 'New Road' appeared, the present Romney Road.)

Ill. 86 The third scheme includes drawings dated 1711. Here the court is flanked only by extensions of the colonnades, leading to the most remarkable of the chapel designs. The road again passes under it, and except in the tunnel itself is opened out to about eighty feet with even wider oval enclosures on either *Ill. 84* side. The chapel is in the form of a Greek cross within a square, *Ill. 72* surrounded by a Doric peristyle, supporting a concave-sided attic, circular drum and hemispherical dome. Its Doric massiveness, its resemblances to Bramante in the simplicity of the dome,

85 'Second' project for Greenwich Hospital. Reconstruction from north-west

to Michelangelo in the pediments resting on triglyphs and to Borromini in the concave attic walls, all would have added up to the simplest and most monumentally plastic object Hawksmoor ever conceived. It would also, like the other chapel projects, have invited comparison with Wren's St Paul's, a building of greater size and greater complexity of form but less obviously and directly dramatic.

Ill. 72

Hawksmoor resurrected and revised the first and third schemes in the period 1723–8, and some of the plans show signs of extensive reworking with pen, brush and even scissors and paste. But the printed *Remarks* of 1728 and the plan attached make no mention of the grand chapel. It must have been obvious by then that no authority was prepared to raise money for such a building, though it is impossible to say whether he was aware of its further implications; these, rather than the inviolability of the Queen's House and the expense of the building, were perhaps ultimately the reasons why it could not be built. A chapel of such monumentality, as the centrepiece of the Hospital, would have inescapably evoked associations of Rome, Popery, and unlimited power whether religious or secular, associations distasteful to every loyal English Protestant. It was proper for the chapel to face the hall, as at Chelsea, as in the post-Reformation Wadham College, for in a lay community religion should know its proper place and not exceed it. The Invalides of Louis XIV was the model, in human terms, for both Chelsea and Greenwich. In the central placing of the two churches of the Invalides, in which the names of God and Louis are architecturally writ large, the French hospital was clearly not the model for the English ones.

Until the building of the railways the most convenient approach to Greenwich was by the river: it is still the most impressive. From the riverside court, flanked by the King Charles and Queen Anne blocks, the colonnades would have quite obscured the southern court but closely framed the chapel. The spectator would have had to pass into the narrows of the colonnades and through most of their length before he could see the form and extent of the court, which would then appear dramatically wide as he reached it. Greenwich today is one of the grandest English buildings of any period; Hawksmoor would have made it also a great spatial experience.

The Commissioners for the Fifty New Churches laid considerable emphasis on steeples and porticoes and on open sites; the churches were to be monuments as well as places of worship (p. 106). On a plan of a site in Bethnal Green, which the Commission never bought, Hawksmoor worked out a setting for a church that would be spatially, monumentally and liturgically effective. The site plan was made in November 1711 and it is reasonably certain that his elaborations, with the annotated plan of a hypothetical church and its setting, were added during the next few months. The drawing is titled 'The Basilica after the Primitive Christians' with a reference to the 'purest times of Christianity' in the fourth century, and many features relate to ecclesiological investigations of the time. These and the plan of the church itself will be discussed in the context of the other church plans (p. 106); its setting is relevant here. The plan shows 'The Church East and West' standing inside the 'septum or Enclosure . . . to keep off filth Nastyness & Brutes', which is simply a rectangular enclosing wall. In the corners of the enclosure are small houses for the minister and

Ill. 87

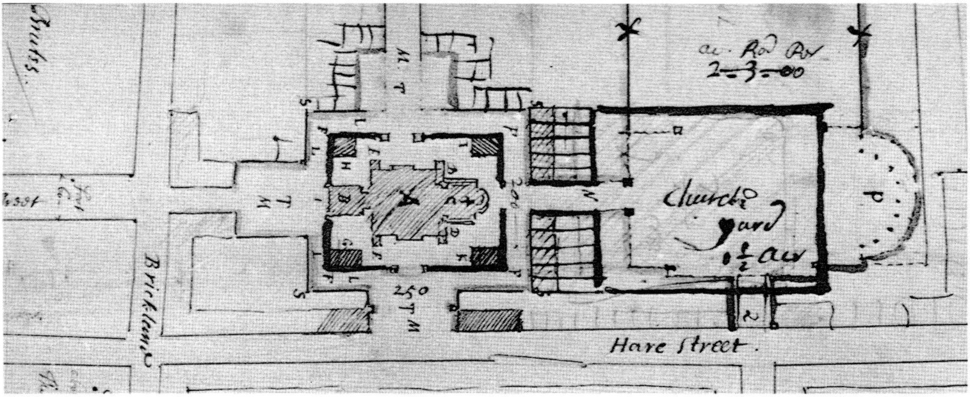

87 Project for a 'Basilica after the Primitive Christians'

church officers; the centre of each side wall is opened except the west, which is occupied by the entrance to the church through the tower. Beyond the enclosure is a further 'open place round ye Church 30 Fot wide' with broad approaches; those on the north and west lead to axially placed streets while that on the south is so broad as to open the whole side of the church to Hare Street. The east approach leads to the 'cemetery, Sleeping place or place of Sepulture' at the east end of which is a hemicycle with columns, described as 'the part relateing to ye Minister, vaulted, and a Cloyster for inscriptions'. The church is thus isolated from surrounding buildings (except the four little houses) by wide expanses, but at the same time it is axially related to them by the lines of the approach streets. On a smaller scale than Greenwich or the universities, Hawksmoor envisaged his building with a complete environment to guide the beholder and enhance his experience. Even on this limited scale, however, he did not manage in any executed work to obtain such a measure of control over surroundings. The Bethnal Green plan, interesting in itself, is also evidence of the purposeful thought he devoted to both the exterior and the interior symmetry of the churches which, in the period 1712–30, he not only imagined but also brought to completion and which still form the core of his work.

CHAPTER FIVE

Achievement

The fifty or so churches rebuilt in the City of London after the Great Fire of 1666 were the first large-scale manifestation of church-building since before the Reformation. The new churches were on the old sites, often small, cramped or irregular; in some cases other buildings hid them from the street. In many cases the shape of the site was the result of a gradual accretion of aisles and chapels. The Church of England in the seventeenth century required in each church only one altar or communion table, reasonably emphasized by decoration; no chapels were wanted. It was also important that the minister should be seen and heard from every part of the interior. This large and urgent building programme was under the general control of Wren, but many details and even some whole churches were only nominally his work. Architecturally he was mainly concerned with the ordering and geometrical division of the interior spaces and the provision of towers with spires or steeples to appear on the London skyline and advertise the prestige of the City and the location of the churches.

Forty years later the City churches were complete, furnished and in use; only a few steeples remained unfinished. The tax on coal coming into London, which had paid for them and for the new St Paul's, could, if imposed for a further period, be utilized to pay for something else. When the roof of St Alfege, Greenwich, fell in on 28 November 1710 the parishioners sent a petition to Parliament suggesting that there might be some money left over from the old tax which could be used to rebuild their church. This was one of the reasons for the Act of Parliament of 1711 for the building of fifty new churches in or near the Cities of London and Westminster or their suburbs; the other reasons were the rapid growth of the Cities (the

88 London. St George-in-the-East. South-west doorcase

capitals of trade and government respectively), consequent concern among churchmen at the lack of churches in the new areas and the proliferation of dissenting chapels in the East End, and the return to power in 1710, after a long period of opposition, of the Tories, who were also the High Church party. The fifty churches it was hoped to build, a round figure that invited comparison with the post-Fire number, would thus be both a work of piety and social improvement and a political and religious commemoration. The Act established a Commission, which included Wren, Vanbrugh and Archer and a number of prominent churchmen and laymen; at its second meeting, on 10 October 1711, the Commission appointed Hawksmoor and William Dickinson, his colleague in the Office of Works, as Surveyors. They were to find and survey sites, treat for their purchase, obtain artificers, make estimates, record the progress of work both for payment and for the information of the Commissioners, and to see in general that designs were carried out correctly and soundly. As administrative architects they were not required to design the churches, although they were in a favourable position when the Commission came to consider designs. Dickinson took up another post in 1713 without realizing any of his designs; Gibbs, who succeeded him, achieved St Mary-le-Strand before being deprived of office in January 1716 as a Papist and a Jacobite and replaced by John James. A month earlier, as a consequence of the succession of George I and the return of the Whigs to power in 1714, a totally new Commission had been appointed; this body included no architects, was wary of everything done by its predecessor, and evidently considered the whole scheme an encumbrance, of whose motivation it disapproved but which it was legally obliged to see through. This decline of enthusiasm, combined with the expensive grandeur of the earlier designs, resulted in the ultimate completion not of fifty but of twelve churches and the payment for three others built independently by outlying parishes. By December 1715 Hawksmoor had four of his own designs under construction, and whether on account of their costliness or for some other reason he seems to have feared for his Surveyorship. He obtained letters of support from the Duchess of Marlborough – who commended his good stewardship – and the Duke of Manchester. He and James remained in office until the virtual winding up of the Commission in 1733; by that time Hawksmoor had produced two more churches, James one, and both in collaboration two others.

We have several kinds of evidence about the ideas embodied in the Fifty New Churches scheme in general and Hawksmoor's churches in particular. This chapter deals as much with the latter as a group of works as with five of them singly; Christ Church and the two joint designs will be discussed later (pp. 141, 189). The 1711 Act provided for the purchase of churchyards (indicating space round the churches), for the use of 'stone and other proper materials' (implying a certain standard of expense and dignity) and for 'Towers or Steeples to each' (like the City Churches of Wren). Two of the Commissioners are known to have set down in writing their views amplifying the conditions of the Act: Wren's 'Letter to a Friend' on the Commission and Vanbrugh's 'Proposals' have both been printed in the modern literature. Wren's remarks are mainly practical, with a recommendation of his St James, Piccadilly as beautiful, convenient and cheap. This type of three-aisled church of five bays with galleries, a western tower and a short chancel on the east, was on the whole too plain for the Commission's architects; in particular Archer's two churches and those of Hawksmoor conformed with Vanbrugh's stress on 'the most Solemn & Awfull Appearance both without and within' and on the grandeur and magnificence of the occasion – one that, whatever its artistic scope, must have displeased him politically since he was an outspoken Whig. The differences between the two documents, which it is customary to emphasize, should not be allowed to obscure the number of points they have in common. Both recommend open or detached sites, towers with spires, and porticoes. Both desire a restricted number of

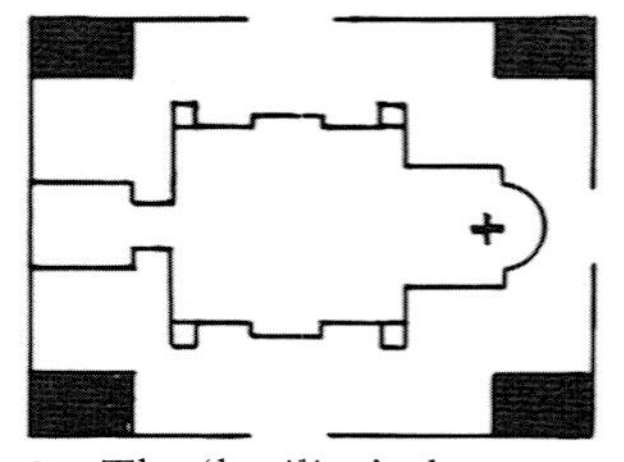
89 The 'basilica' plan

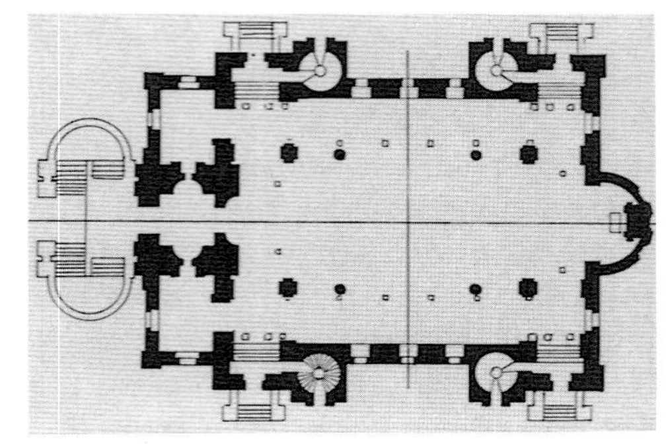
90 St George-in-the-East. Plan

pews, so that those with no title to pew seats might be accommodated elsewhere. Both condemn burials in or near churches; this practice was forbidden by one of the clauses in the supplementary Act of 1712.

The emphasis on steeples, porticoes and open sites is reflected in a resolution of the Commission of July 1712, which also dealt with several liturgical features including the provision of a chancel raised by three steps at the east end – it had previously been agreed that all the churches should be correctly oriented. Vanbrugh's epithet, 'handsome', was used in connection with the porticoes. The Commission made a further curious provision for 'one general design or Forme' to be agreed upon for all the churches excepting the towers and steeples; subsequent discussion led to no agreement and the idea lapsed. It was, however, at the time of these preliminary discussions about the form, features and arrangement of the churches, and in the light of them, that Hawksmoor produced the hypothetical 'Basilica' plan already mentioned. This plan, which also bears a note about 'No burying in ye church', is partly a historical reconstruction, partly an ideal 'model' for a new church; moreover, each of these functions is considered both ecclesiologically and architecturally. The use of the crypt (or 'Vaults') for a charity school relates to Hawksmoor's own time, the seclusion of the side galleries for women refers to the Early Christians, and the provision in the west porch of a font for baptism by immersion is connected both with ideas of early practice and with a clause in the July 1712 resolution, that fonts should be large enough for 'dipping' if it was desired. The

Ills. 87, 89

church is not a *basilica* in the normal architectural sense of a building with colonnaded aisles and an apse; except for the rather larger chancel and the eastern vestries it is very like St George-in-the-East in plan. Side galleries as extra accommodation (rather than as a means of dividing the sexes) are a common feature of post-Reformation churches, but they interfere with the symmetry of a church planned on intersecting axes. If Hawksmoor had in mind Hagia Sofia (known in

Ill. 90

Ill. 91

91 St George-in-the-East. Interior in 1940

92 Thomas Archer. St Paul, Deptford. Interior

England from Grelot's *Voyage to Constantinople* published in 1683) he could find there an ancient precedent for side galleries clearly separated from the rest of the interior. In fact he never achieved such a separation, and the nearest to it in plan (though quite different in spatial feeling from a Byzantine building) is Archer's St Paul, Deptford, in which the galleries are like outsize theatre boxes, isolated by the corner staircases. Archer's church was begun in 1713, and in the atmosphere of the Commission office at that time it is certain that many ideas were freely exchanged.

Ills. 92, 93

Archer's two churches and Hawksmoor's six are all planned around intersecting axes; Hawksmoor's in particular are based on straight lines and rectangles. This means that their relation to the circular or oval centrally planned churches of the Renaissance and Baroque – and even to those on a Greek cross plan of four equal arms – is visibly limited and genetically indirect. It is thus unlikely that a single source can be found for Hawksmoor's and Archer's axial plans; several lines of descent, however, were open. Late seventeenth-century inquiry into the form of early Christian buildings (an inquiry that had begun with early Reformation emphasis on primitive observances) undoubtedly provided one line. A second was the historical interest of Wren and his circle in pre-Gothic and pre-Classical styles, or those outside the current norms of Western architecture. A third line was the general interest of architects from the Renaissance onwards in centralized buildings, from Brunelleschi to Borromini, J.H. Mansart and Fischer von Erlach. This interest is manifested elsewhere in Hawksmoor's work and in many aspects of Wren's (p. 198); not the least significant were the germinal idea of St Paul's as a domed crossing and the plan, probably deriving from Dutch Protestant examples, of a Greek cross within a square for some of the City Churches. A further line was the importance of the transverse axis in such interior spaces as the hall of Castle Howard and in the corridor planning of that house and Blenheim. Finally, the importance of axial planning and of changes of direction has already been examined in Hawksmoor's environment plans and in the early house plans.

Ills. 114, 180

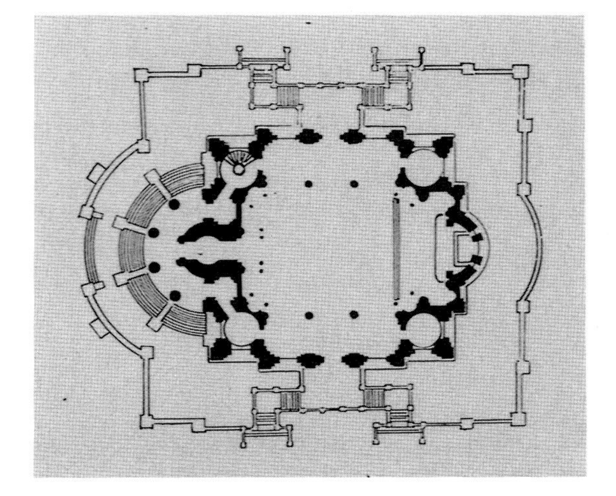

93 Thomas Archer. St Paul, Deptford. Plan

The first church was appropriately enough the rebuilding of St Alfege, Greenwich, begun in 1712 and finished structurally in 1714; the Commission even decided to begin this church before agreeing on the general model for the others. It has an eastern portico behind the chancel, and it appears from the Commission minutes of 6 August that porticoes at both ends had been suggested, that the chosen design was the smaller of two offered by Hawksmoor, and that the absence of any internal pillars was considered noteworthy – as indeed it is in a span of 65 feet by 90 feet. It is significant of the climate of the Commission at the time that four weeks earlier the minutes mention Hawksmoor's design as 'improved' by Archer, but we have no idea what the improvements were nor whether the design was the one finally adopted in August. The Commissioners also attempted during building to leave out, for economy, the external north and south porches which also house staircases to the galleries, but Hawksmoor managed to convince them that the porches were inexpensive or indispensable. One important feature of his design, the tower, was not executed but is known from Kip's 1714 engraving. The vestry's petitions for a steeple led in 1723 to a sharp reply from the Commissioners; disenchanted with the programme inherited from the original Commission, they stated – in the face of the 1711 Act – that it was not their business to erect steeples. Only in 1730, after a further campaign of petitions, did they agree to the construction of James's visually rather inadequate recasing of the medieval tower; by then Hawksmoor had translated the original design to the north bank of the Thames.

Ill. 96

Ill. 95

Ill. 94

Ill. 105

The portico was put at the east to face the main street; the arch rising into the pediment is a late Roman motif which was most readily available to Hawksmoor in Wren's projects for St Paul's – the Great Model transepts and a discarded design for a giant west portico. The Doric order of Hawksmoor's portico is continued all round the church in pilasters. It is the only one of his churches to receive this treatment, and it is tempting to wonder whether Archer, who dealt very similarly

94 St Alfege, Greenwich. Reconstruction with projected steeple

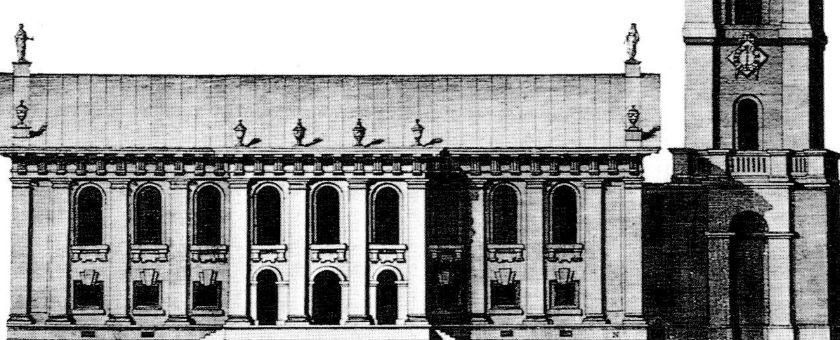

95 St Alfege. Engraving, 1714

with St John, Smith Square, 'improved' Hawksmoor's design in this way; without a continuous order St Alfege would have resembled the Clarendon Building, begun in the same year and having the same complex cutting back into the wall in layers. *Ills. 52, 99*

The interior of St Alfege is a single great room with a very shallow chancel recess made to look deeper by illusionist painting. *Ill. 101* It has long since lost the great plaster 'middle flower' of the ceiling, seven by six feet, and the fittings have been more than once rearranged. Originally the pulpit and desk stood on either side in front of the chancel arch, and there was a wide aisle between the pews across the church from one porch to the other, as well as the aisle from tower to chancel. Thus in the floor layout and the 'floating' ceiling there was originally better definition of the centre lines and centre point of the interior; its apparently deliberate spatial ambiguity was more selective and less confused when the church was consecrated in 1718 than it is now.

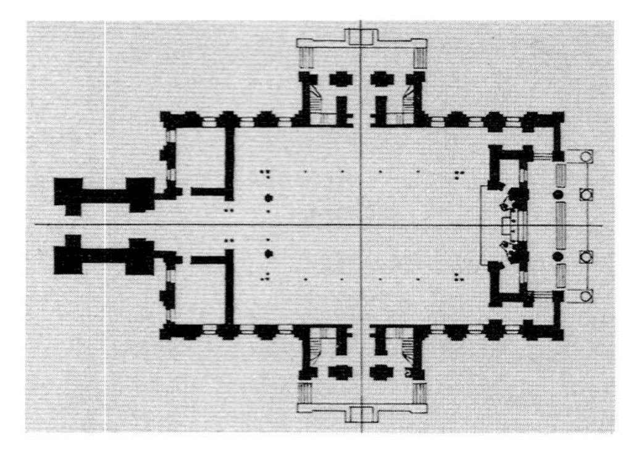

96 St Alfege. Plan

97 St Alfege from south-east

98 St Alfege. East portico

9 (*below right*) St Alfege. Detail of wall
00 (*bottom right*) St Alfege. Roman altar

101 St Alfege, Greenwich. Interior

102 St George-in-the-East. First design. West front

St George-in-the-East, in Upper Wapping or Wapping Stepney, is one of the three Stepney churches begun in 1714; it was built almost concurrently with St Anne, Limehouse, and the two seem to have been linked in the architect's mind while the third, Christ Church, Spitalfields (p. 141) was separate in conception and evolution. The site of St George-in-the-East was already confined on the south by houses, and Hawksmoor tried in vain to get the Commission to buy four of them for demolition in order to open the south elevation to the street known as the Highway. With this intention, as with some features of the plan, he probably had the 'Primitive Christian' design in mind. The surviving drawings for St George show that the design evolved gradually; the foundations were laid in 1714 and the church roofed in 1717, but the form of the silhouette above the roof was only finalized in the latter year. The tower had started as a two-stage belfry with an octagonal 'pepper-pot' and there were no turrets over the gallery staircases. The latter first appear in embryo as additions to a later elevation, dated August 1714; the additions also include the

Ill. 87
Ill. 102
Ill. 103

103 St George-in-the-East. Intermediate design. West front

104 St George-in-the-East
from south-west

suggestion of a stepped pyramidal roof, probably of lead-covered wood and reverting to Hawksmoor's first idea for a plain pyramid enclosing an unlit hemispherical dome. He seems to have remained undecided about the form of the roof itself until the end of 1716, and one drawing has a curious note

to the effect that 'If what Mr Groves [the carpenter] has provided for Waping Stepney Cannot Serve at Limehouse – then we must be content to put it upon Wapping Church'. In 1717 the west and east pediments of St George, and coves to support the turrets, had to be keyed into the masonry and

105 St George-in-the-East from south-east

part of the parapet already built was dismantled to accommodate them. The tower acquired a third belfry stage and the lantern became an open octagon, derived from the unexecuted Greenwich one; the square triglyph finials were replaced by fluted cylindrical ones with swags, variations in a different context of the four 'Roman altars' that stand outside the east end of Greenwich church. The staircase turrets, which had first appeared as simple cylinders, were also gradually transformed into much taller buttressed octagons carrying small versions of the original 'pepper-pot' capped by lead domes and bronze flaming urns.

Ill. 100

From the west the tower appears to burst upwards from the ground, splitting the pediment in two with a force we usually associate with the soaring lines of Gothic towers; yet the conscious origins of Hawksmoor's towers do not seem to be Gothic. In the case of St Anne, Limehouse, the derivation is more demonstrably not Gothic but classical. The earliest drawings already show a circular western portico like a baptistery, half within and half outside the façade, and forming part of the support for the tower, but the tower supports a heavy prismatic lantern somewhat like Hawksmoor's *Proposition IV* for the Queen's College. This was then reduced to a simple octagonal capped lantern, a form Hawksmoor elsewhere associated with the Tower of the Winds (p. 151); groups of piers were added on the diagonals, and the pyramidal pinnacles last of all in the sequence of drawings. The steeple as a form is a Gothic invention, and Hawksmoor no doubt had in mind some of the great medieval English towers, but he arrived at the forms of the two Stepney steeples wholly by means of Renaissance or Antique detail. That they remind us of Gothic steeples is incidental; the architect considered them entirely appropriate to the other classical details of the churches. When at the same date (1716) he built up forms that are, in abstract terms, very similar, but for a 'Gothic' ensemble at All Souls, he used medievalizing details. The basic forms are clothed in a style to fit their context.

Ill. 104

Ills. 112, 113

Ill. 57

Ill. 107

Ill. 106

106 Oxford.
All Souls. Tower

107 St Anne, Limehouse
Intermediate design
for steeple

108 (*below*) St Anne,
Limehouse.
First design.
North elevation

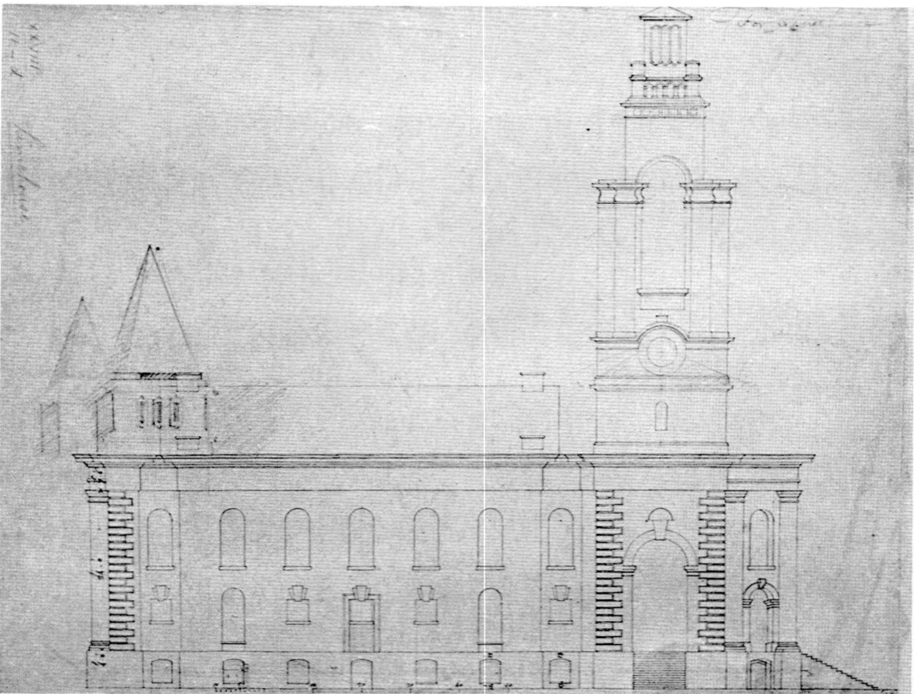

109 St Anne, Limehouse, from north-west

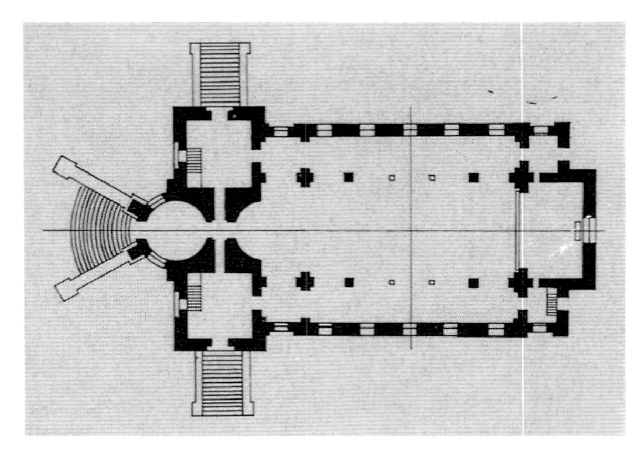

110 St Anne, Limehouse. Plan

112 St Anne. West front

111 (*below*) St Anne. Interior

In plan both St George and St Anne are Greek crosses within rectangles, St Anne being not square but slightly longer from west to east than across. In both churches the rectangle-cross area is flanked by extra eastern and western bays to which Hawksmoor referred as wings and which he considered distinguishing externally by a lower roof. St George is ceiled (or

Ill. 110

113 St Anne. Porch. Interior

was – it was gutted in 1941 and in reconstruction the interior has been altered) with intersecting plaster barrel-vaults of extremely depressed section and flat corner pieces. St Anne has a flat ceiling with beams marking the corners and a central circular moulding. Both are formal devices to emphasize the centralized feeling of the interiors and to give the impression of a wide covering which floats as weightlessly as the great oval panel at Greenwich. Neither church can be entered on the transverse axis; the north and south side doors of St George and the east and west doors of St Anne lead to the 'wings', and the central space has to be experienced first of all from some point outside it. The ambiguity between the centralized plan and the emphasis on the west–east axis made by the galleries reflects a conflict, which Hawksmoor could not resolve, between formal considerations and the requirements of the Anglican liturgy. However, the latter were by no means as clear-cut as the requirements of either the Roman Church of

Ill. 91
Ill. 111
Ill. 101

the seventeenth century or the Anglican Church of the nineteenth. The communion table was not the only focal point of the church; liturgically speaking it would be nearer the truth to say that there was a focal area that included the altar, the pulpit and the reading desk. Thus particular or exclusive emphasis on the chancel was neither appropriate nor desirable, and Hawksmoor in fact treated each of his interiors differently according to its shape, its religious character and its external situation. That he was capable of clear central planning is evident from the Mausoleum at Castle Howard and from some of the designs for the Radcliffe Library, such as a plan based (by way of Grelot) on the Suleimaniyeh at Constantinople; in the special circumstances of the churches he adopted special devices. This is nowhere better evident than in the two churches begun in 1716.

Ills. 114, 115

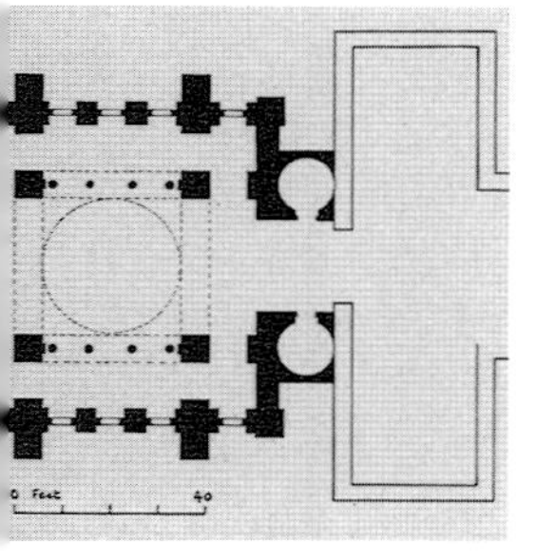

114 Early project for the Radcliffe Camera. Plan

115 Early project for the Radcliffe Camera. Elevation

Neither St Mary Woolnoth nor St George, Bloomsbury, was built on an open site. Old St Mary Woolnoth had suffered comparatively little damage in the Great Fire and had been patched up under Wren; by 1712 it was very decrepit and the supplementary Act of that year allowed for its rebuilding from the surplus of the old coal tax. The site was open to the street on the north and west; the south wall could only be seen in steep foreshortening until the construction of King William Street in the nineteenth century (it was more effectively obscured in 1900 by the outworks of Bank Underground Station). Hawksmoor therefore treated the elevations differently. The south wall is plain with deeply recessed upper and lower windows, strongly projecting sills to the latter, blind recesses below them, and rugged lintels and keystones to the basement apertures. The north wall has instead of windows three rusticated niches which enshrined concave aedicules – in much the same way as Hawksmoor elsewhere elevated forms on bases or pedestals. In the west front the breadth of the Stepney churches is now achieved by a fusion of twin towers into a single mass. Outside and inside St Mary is the smallest of the churches; inside it is also the simplest and most nearly logical. A central square defined by triplets of Corinthian columns supports a clerestory or lantern whose four big lunettes provide most of the light. The galleries have been removed and their carved fronts fixed to the side walls, but old views show that originally they were subordinate to the visual structure of the tripled columns. Because of its compactness this is still the most powerful of the churches.

Ill. 116
Ill. 119
Ill. 172

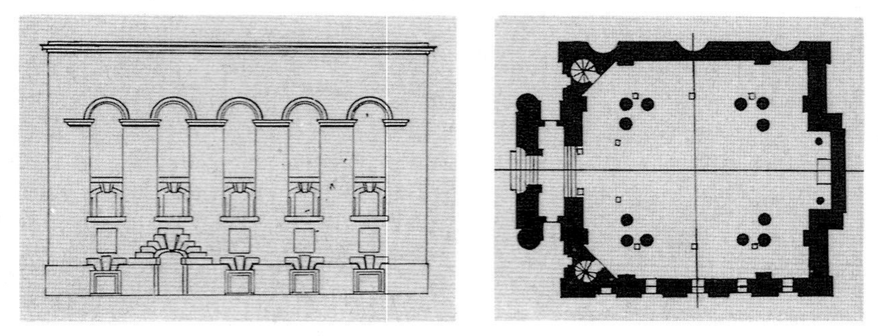

116, 117 St Mary Woolnoth. South wall elevation and plan

118 St Mary Woolnoth. West front before 1900

119 St Mary Woolnoth.
Niche on north side

120 St Mary Woolnoth.
Interior before alteration

121 St Mary Woolnoth.
North side

122 St Mary Woolnoth. Interior

123 Project for St George, Bloomsbury

124 St George, Bloomsbury from south

The most complex of the churches, St George, Bloomsbury, had the most difficult site, narrow from west to east, deep from north to south and edged with houses, some of which were subsequently demolished. The first hypothetical plan of November 1711 was prophetically like St Mary Woolnoth; the second, a year later, had a west tower and eastern apse much like the final building. By the summer of 1716 when the site had been acquired and work began the design had undergone many changes, including in 1715 a decision to build a church designed by Vanbrugh with the altar on the north as it 'cannot conveniently be built any other way'. Hawksmoor, however, had more than one idea for the other way, for one of the few drawings connected with the church shows an oval design, related to the Queen's College sketches (p. 73), which would fit the site with an eastern altar. It may have been his skill in meeting the liturgical brief which finally won the day for his design against Vanbrugh's. In both the oval design and the

Ill. 123

HOTEL

final one entrance was possible from the west, so that one faced the altar along the short axis. The church has been seriously altered and it is now very difficult to appreciate the original *Ill. 127* effect.

Hawksmoor's brief must have included the provision of access both from Hart Street (now Bloomsbury Way) on the *Ill. 125* south and on the north from Little Russell Street and the new residential area beyond, which formed an important part of the parish. He therefore provided steps up to the tower on both sides, to an entrance intended to have equal importance to the southern one through the portico; the latter led the spectator in on the long axis but quite clearly on the side of the church, *Ill. 126* under one gallery and facing another. The parishioners found their church inconvenient from the start, and in 1781 the interior was rearranged with the altar on the north; subse-

125 St George, Bloomsbury. North front

127 St George, Bloomsbury. Interior looking north-east ▶

126 St George, Bloomsbury. Plan

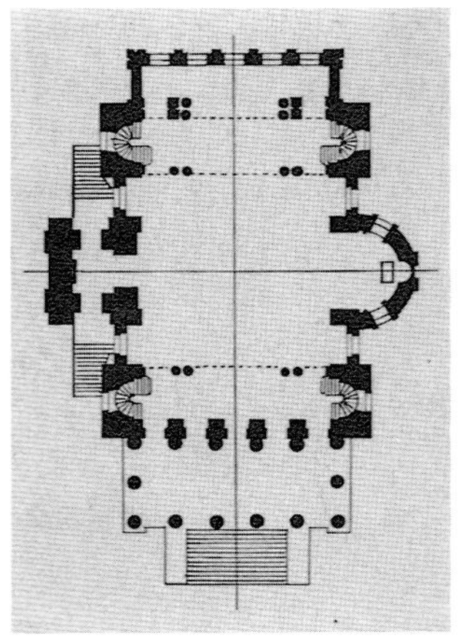

quently the tower entrance was blocked, and for a time the plasterwork of the eastern apse was boxed in. The big wooden altar niche now on the north side appears to be the original, moved from the apse and quite out of place. The 1781 alterations included the removal of the north gallery; one of the mysteries of the church is the extent of this gallery and the function of the northernmost bay. If the survey plan in an extra-illustrated Pennant's *London* (Westminster Public Library) records the original state, the gallery was an exact counterpart to the southern one and the northern bay was open behind it and used as a kind of baptistery; the doubling of the arch and piers at the front of this bay can still be explained as necessary support for the roof system.

What the alterations to St George, Bloomsbury most obscure is its original state of balance between two ways of approach and two axes; this balance is now reflected most clearly in the differences in horizontal and vertical stress between the north and south walls and the east and west, and in the arrangement of the ceiling mouldings to form rectangles in line with both axes.

In the treatment of the front wall and the hexastyle portico Hawksmoor seems again to have remembered his Queen's

128 John James. London. St George, Hanover Square

129 St George, Bloomsbury. Steeple

College project. But this was not an isolated example either of grand columnar architecture or of a belated literal response to the suggestion of porticoes. In the early 1720s Gibbs's St Martin-in-the-Fields (not one of the Fifty New Churches), James's St George, Hanover Square and Hawksmoor's Bloomsbury church were all under construction with hexastyle porticoes, and must all have had a common source either in the Commission office about 1711–12 or in Wren's circle a few years earlier. The pilastered treatment of Greenwich Church, Gibbs's unexecuted models for peripteral churches and Hawksmoor's project for an Oxford church (p. 93) may likewise go back to the same source in Wren's interest in historical architecture.

Ill. 128

The same atmosphere accounts for the steeple of the Bloomsbury church. A model of this was made in 1723 just before its construction began, and Hawksmoor quite possibly had not

Ill. 129

previously decided on its final form. The stepped pyramid on columns is based, though less correctly than in a number of hypothetical drawings, on Pliny's account of the Tomb of Mausolus at Halicarnassus, a monument of which Hawksmoor knew – and elsewhere illustrated – Wren's written reconstruction. His delight in putting objects on pedestals here reached its peak, for he converted the free reconstruction of this Wonder of the Ancient world into an enormous royal hatchment or coat of arms: the lifesize lion and unicorn fighting for the crown appeared in Portland stone on the north and south faces. They were taken down in 1871 as 'very doubtful ornaments' in bad repair and only the crowns remain, but the statue of the king (George I) survives on a Roman altar at the top of the pyramid.

Ill. 133

The existence of the Commission records and of many original drawings makes it possible to trace in detail the creation of the Hawksmoor churches – his most considerable group of works – and in many instances almost to watch him at work. The presence of Vanbrugh and Archer on the original Commission raises the question of their possible influence or interference, but it is almost impossible to find firm evidence of either: the note 'Mr Vanbrugh in Duke [Street]' on one drawing is less telling than might appear, since the Vanbrugh known to have lodged there was cousin William, Secretary of Greenwich Hospital. The plainness and 'noble simplicity' of the Stepney and Bloomsbury churches are, as much as the fastidious placing and sizing of windows and other features on the wall surfaces, the true successors of the Writing School and the Queen Anne Block at Greenwich. They differ from Easton Neston, Castle Howard and Blenheim as much as do Vanbrugh's later houses, but they represent another man's change of course in the second decade of the eighteenth century. Hawksmoor came nearest to the picturesqueness of Vanbrugh's King's Weston and Seaton Delaval in the Gothick of All Souls. And the details of the churches, almost purely architectural rather than sculptural, maintain the scholarly feeling for form

130 St Anne, Limehouse. East end

that is Hawksmoor's alone: the attics over the east end of St Anne, Limehouse, the niches of St Mary Woolnoth and the doorways of St George-in-the-East which derive both from Wren, in the oval windows, and from Michelangelo, in the triglyphs used as imposts.

Ill. 130

Ill. 88

CHAPTER SIX

Reform

The steeple of Christ Church, Spitalfields, finished in 1729, was rebuilt in the nineteenth century without the three dormer windows on each face, the flame-like 'crockets' running up the corners, and the large stone finial at the top, which made it originally more a suggestion and less a copy of a Gothic broach spire, and closer in spirit to one of the designs based on the Mausoleum of Halicarnassus. Christ Church was begun in 1714, but it was not until 1723–4, when the body of the church was complete, that Hawksmoor replaced the original idea of a flat front, a plain box-like tower and a little octagonal lantern with the majestic portico and tower that comprise the greater part of the western aspect today. He had decided earlier to use a Venetian window – an arched opening between two rectangular ones, one of the chief Palladian trade-marks – at the east end of the church. When he came to the west end he transformed the motif into a portico, wrapping the lead roof around the architrave. On this enormous scale the motif is less like a window and more like the eastern portico of Greenwich church; nevertheless its Palladian derivation is clear, and because of its transformation the motif belongs to Hawksmoor's stock of symbolic architectural images. Moreover, the Venetian window motif is repeated higher up in the belfry stage, on the same scale and with an obvious parallelism of form so close as to offend the canons of academic architecture.

Ill. 132
Ill. 133
Ill. 134
Ill. 131

It is difficult and often dangerous to select a particular event or a particular year as the decisive one that will stand in history for a complex and protracted pattern of human action. However, if the 'Glorious Revolution' of 1688 represents the final replacement of absolutist monarchy in Britain by a constitutional monarchy responsible to Parliament, the year 1715

131 Christ Church, Spitalfields. West front

132 Christ Church, Spitalfields. West front before alteration

133 Project for a church

may stand for the principal campaign in the architectural revolution that replaced English Baroque by neo-Palladianism. The Whig philosopher the third Earl of Shaftesbury's *Letter concerning design*, written and circulated in 1712, attacked French taste and influence, and in particular the absolute, king-like, monopoly Wren had exercised over public architecture. He named St Paul's and Hampton Court among the disastrous fruits of this monopoly, and he went on to attack by clear implication Blenheim and the Fifty New Churches as successors to it. He claimed that a self-determining people would determine and realize, among other things, its own national style, but he was not very explicit about its character.

On this foundation built the Scottish architect, Colin Campbell, who arrived in London about 1711. He failed to ingratiate himself with the Fifty New Churches Commission but succeeded in gaining a number of private patrons for himself. In 1715 he published the first volume of *Vitruvius Britannicus*, a compendium of plates of contemporary architecture including several of his own designs and prefaced by a manifesto for the national style. A few months later London saw the first part of an allied publication: the first English translation of Palladio's *Quattro libri dell'architettura*, by James Leoni, offered the documentary support that was needed. Campbell attacked not Wren and his school but their models, Bernini, Borromini, Fontana and 'Things that are foreign' in general. His praise was reserved for the remoter (in time and spirit) academic Renaissance style of Palladio and above all for his acknowledged British follower, Inigo Jones; the very title

134 Christ Church. Early design. South side

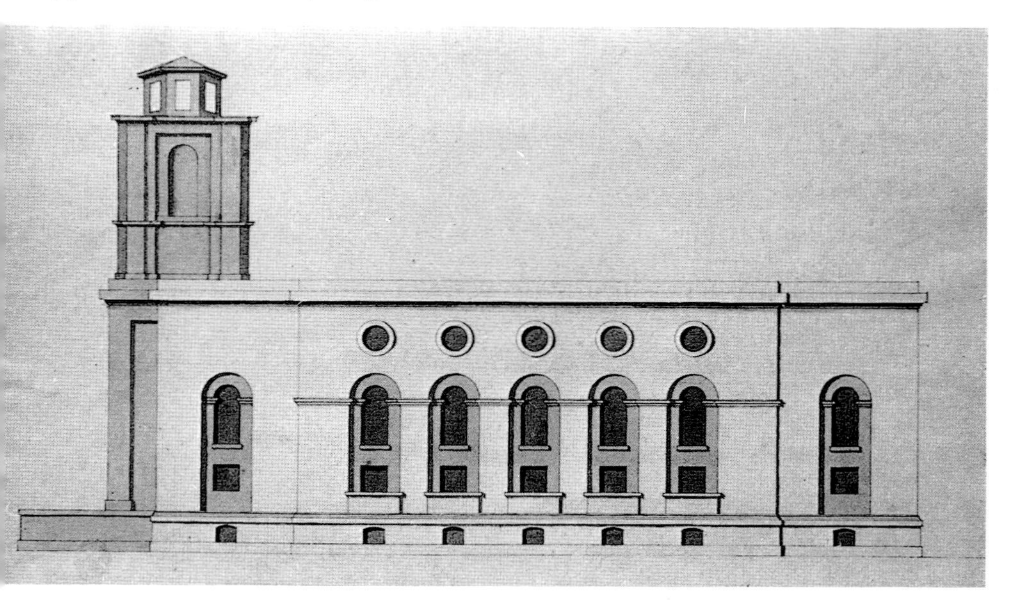

of his book, 'The British Vitruvius', had been coined to describe Jones himself. Campbell's aim was – apart from his own advancement – to put the clock back to before the whole Baroque interlude of the Wren school: to take up the thread where Jones had left it and give to Britain a kind of prolonged latter-day High Renaissance based on the rules of Antiquity, Reason and Taste.

Campbell's extraordinary success in promoting his ideas was due to several factors: his skill as a publicist, his ability in personal politics, the timing of his campaign, the enthusiasm (after 1715) of the third Earl of Burlington, the personal disgrace of the Marlboroughs and public reaction to the ostentation of Blenheim, the expensive fantasy of some of the new churches, the ideas of a simple style suggested by Shaftesbury and by men like John James (p. 58), and not least the lack of effective opposition. The Wren school was vulnerable in two respects, both consequences of Wren's command of the Royal Works. The liberal attitude he had shown to the ideas of younger colleagues like Vanbrugh and Hawksmoor enabled them to bloom as artistic personalities and still to contribute to the progress of the Works. The Wren school was thus a school of individualists, whose force came from separate personalities and not at all from *esprit de corps*; there was no party line in the face of attack. When Vanbrugh and Hawksmoor were under fire over Castle Howard in 1724, Hawksmoor's reply to Lord Carlisle was to the effect that they too followed the Ancients (p. 20). Later attacks on the Mausoleum elicited from Hawksmoor an array of quotations from the theorists to justify his designs to the critics, but he was fortunate to have in Carlisle a patron who understood or at least accepted the real reasons for his decisions (p. 199). But Wren's liberalism, combined with his great age, also meant that minor irregularities could be found and greater ones insinuated in the Works. Vanbrugh had attempted with Carlisle and Lord Halifax to deal with the real, minor ones; by 1718 he had managed to save himself from the chimerical ones but to save no others:

135 Christ Church. Interior

Wren was dismissed, Hawksmoor lost the Secretaryship and the Clerkship of the royal palaces, and Wren's son the post of Clerk Engrosser. They were replaced by the notorious William Benson as Surveyor, his brother Benjamin as Secretary and Campbell, described as his 'agent', as Chief Clerk. Wren had made the Office of Works a loose professional organization which offered no sinecures; within a few years it had become through political influence a haven for gentlemen architects, time-servers, and those who, like Benson, were best qualified by what Hawksmoor called 'extream Need of an employment'. The work of the Office was done by deputies, legitimate but not creative, and the Office survived partly because the early Hanoverian kings began no great new works; the achievements of early Georgian architecture lie in country houses and the London squares.

Hawksmoor viewed the entire Palladian camp with feelings between contempt and hatred. Financially the revolution affected him probably less than, like many men careful with hard-earned money, he habitually claimed. In private practice also his ideas as well as his experience continued to find him employment. But the most significant aspect of the new style in relation to an older artist should be a stylistic one: how much did Palladianism affect him artistically?

It would indeed be surprising if his wide interest in architectural sources had excluded Palladio or, in his later years, the idiomatic vocabulary of English Palladianism. There is considerable visual evidence that he by no means ignored this vocabulary, though the use he made of it was his own. But it is possible to go further, and to see the early eighteenth-century concern with a national style *and* the concern of Hawksmoor, Vanbrugh and (to a lesser extent) Wren with styles as the alternative clothing of basic forms, as different manifestations of a general concern with style as a self-conscious aesthetic activity. When we seek today to distinguish Hawksmoor's style from that of the Palladians we base our investigation on the abstract concepts of art-history of the last hundred years.

136 Christ Church. East end

137 Vanbrugh. Seaton Delaval. South front

138 Project for a palace

Ill. 52

We may say, for example, that Hawksmoor was concerned with the wall as a plastic medium capable of exploration, development or sculptural treatment, and we may even become metaphorical and call it, for him, an organic medium with its own life, in which individual forms grow out of the wall or grow together to compose it. We may say on the contrary that for the Palladians the wall is dead, inert, a medium on to which forms may be fixed but which is not developed in itself. The basis of our distinction is an underlying attitude to the materials and processes of architectural creation. Hawksmoor was without doubt aware of such a distinction of attitude, but with the aesthetic interests and critical terms of his time he could not define it in our terms; his description of his way of following the Ancients (p. 20) is in fact surprisingly modern for the time. His concern with style was one of vocabulary and programme, of details and their combinations suitable for certain types of building and certain associations of ideas. A fuller study than has yet been made of his detailed sources would probably confirm the idea of a gradual change over his career, consistently through the various kinds of building which engaged him at any moment. The year 1715 does not mark any new awareness in Hawksmoor of the diversity of styles; it does however mark approximately the challenge of

new Palladian motifs and also a specific case of a dilemma for him between old and new.

It is noticeable that both Vanbrugh's and Hawksmoor's vocabularies became increasingly attuned towards Renaissance Italy (as opposed to Baroque Rome or France) in the 1710s. In Vanbrugh's work this change is first seen in designs for Eastbury (*c.* 1715) and culminates in Seaton Delaval, begun in 1718; there he used, within a restricted range of motifs, Venetian windows and also rectangular openings with triangular pediments of a pure Cinquecento form. In Hawksmoor's east window at Spitalfields the quotation was equally literal; he also made a number of sketches, too fragmentary to make any reconstruction possible now, for a palace relying heavily on the vocabulary of Jones and Webb. The sketches for the library block of Worcester College, Oxford, of about 1717, which are annotated with his sources, are less specifically Palladian, except for references to Jones's Queen's Chapel at St James's: the angle quoins on a sheet of mouldings are described as 'The Rusticks according to Mr Jones, at St James Chapell'. The Venetian windows in the street front are very similar to the east window of the Queen's Chapel, and Hawksmoor at some date obtained drawings of the latter. Other named sources for the Worcester College design are the

Ill. 137

Ill. 136

Ill. 138

Ill. 139

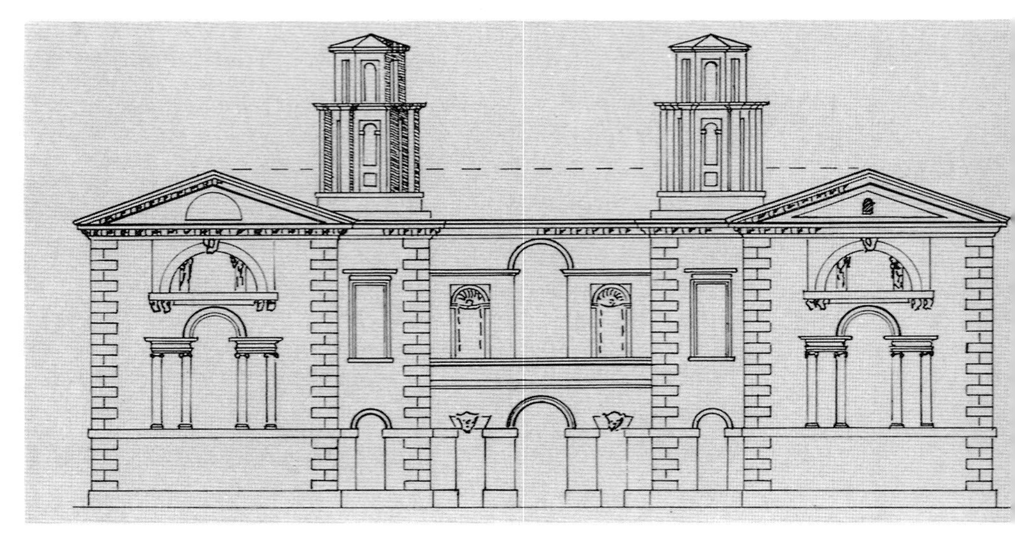

139 Project for street front, Worcester College, Oxford

140 Project for garden front, Worcester College

141 Alternative garden front, Worcester College

ancient Roman arch at Saintes in the Charente, which he knew from François Blondel's *Cours d'Architecture*, the Edifice des Tuteles at Bordeaux (from the plate in Perrault's *Vitruvius*) for the amphorae between the upper windows, the Palazzo Farnese for the aedicules with flanking Ionic columns in the same drawing, and the Pantheon and the Arch of Constantine for mouldings. The towers on the street front are based on the Tower of the Winds in Athens which Hawksmoor, misquoting Vitruvius, calls the 'Tower of Andromachus'. This mixture of Antique and Cinquecento sources can be lengthened by the unnamed borrowing of the end arches surmounted by segmental pediments (from Michelangelo) in the garden front and a generic resemblance between an alternative unbroken Doric elevation for this front and the *palazzo* fronts of Raphael, Peruzzi and Sangallo. The building finally begun in 1720 is a distillation from Hawksmoor's sketches by Clarke and Townesend: it is accomplished and possesses both monumentality and elegance, but as in the case of the Queen's College the building lacks the force of Hawksmoor's original ideas. A comparison of those ideas for the two buildings shows quite clearly the change in his vocabulary in less than a decade.

Ill. 140
Ill. 141
Ills. 55, 1

142 George Clarke and William Townesend.
Oxford. Worcester College. Garden front

The one portion of Greenwich Hospital for which we have documentary proof of Hawksmoor's authorship was built while he was considering Worcester College: the loggias added at the ends of the court in Queen Anne Block. They have some similarity in feeling and treatment with the Worcester designs, but in another sense they are a development of the 'back front' of the Queen Anne Block begun in 1700 and thus have roots further back in his mind. The idea of utilitarian plainness recurs in the brick arcade of Stable Yard at St James's Palace, also of 1716–17, but the element of complexity in the relation of ideas is in fact characteristic, and it may be that even the most literal borrowings were, consciously or unconsciously, more devious than they appear to us. Reference to the back of Queen Anne Block in the context of this later chapter reveals, if it is not already apparent, a motif looking rather like a Venetian window in the centre of the top storey. It is in fact a single round-headed window with small columns supporting the arch instead of imposts, but it is flanked at a distance by rectangular windows, and it seems only a short step to reduce the intervening wall areas to make a three-light group. Hawksmoor indeed invented for himself a form very like the

Ill. 144

Ill. 30

Ill. 143

143 St James's Palace. Stable Yard

144 Greenwich Hospital. Queen Anne Court. North end loggia

Venetian window, which can be found in varying embryonic guises in the first design for Castle Howard (north door), the ends of the Kensington Orangery, the roof-top structures of the Queen's College designs, the attic of a rectangular design for the Radcliffe Library, the belfry of St Anne, Limehouse and in other places. The portico of Greenwich Church, in which the arch breaks into the pediment, is of the same family on a larger scale, and is perhaps the clue to the interest Hawksmoor showed in such motifs. The Italians (for example Scamozzi) used the Venetian window in the centre of a façade to effect a junction between the main vertical axis and the

Ill. 98

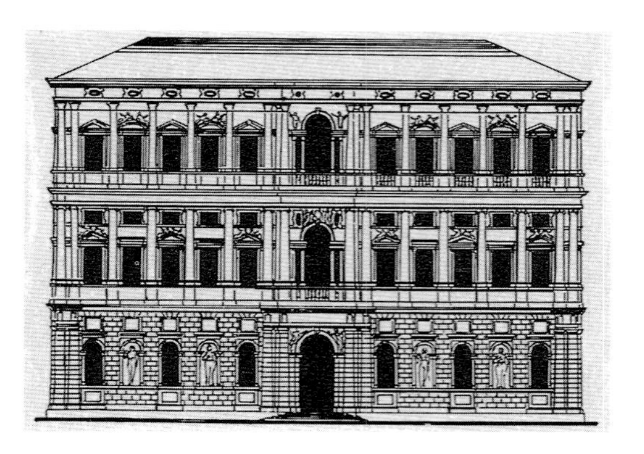

145 Vincenzo Scamozzi. Design for a palace (redrawn)

146 Project for Ockham Park. Garden front

Ill. 145 horizontal line of a row of rectangular windows: that is, at a vital point of a closely knit visual structure. The English Palladians (and Vanbrugh) tended to use the motif as a decorative element applied often to the ends of an elevation and isolated rather than integrated into any visual structure. The common feature of the Hawksmoor examples we have considered is that in each one an arched opening is used to interrupt a continuous line such as a cornice or string course; this both breaks a horizontal (and may thus be called dynamic or disruptive) and also joins vertically two otherwise distinct zones of the elevation. In one case at least, at St Mary Woolnoth, the same device appears on two levels to produce a compound *Ill. 119* motif which departs from the expected elements of the façade in both scale and arrangement; this is analogous to the construction of a solely visual system in, for example, the court front of King William Block at Greenwich. When Hawksmoor turned more literally to Palladio he found that the true Venetian window could also be used the same way, for example *Ill. 123* in the oval design for St George, Bloomsbury; in 1727 he repeated this particular usage in a design for Ockham Park that is composed almost entirely from the Venetian window and the English blocked or 'Gibbs' window, a pseudo-Palladian *Ill. 146* motif which probably derives from Serlio. In both designs a door is crammed in underneath the Venetian window in an unorthodox but quite personal manner. A further surprising discovery is that while the orthodox Venetian windows of

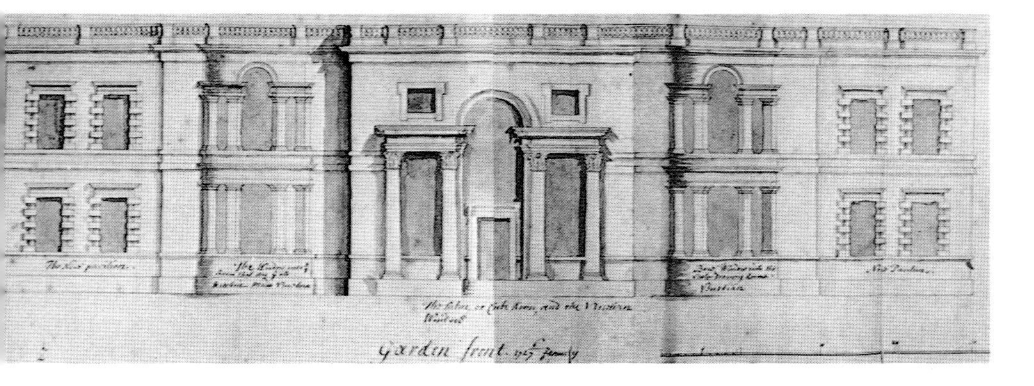

Vanbrugh's Eastbury, several of Hawksmoor's and one of Archer's were designed in or before 1715, and the motif was used frequently by Inigo Jones, it does not occur at all in the first volume of *Vitruvius Britannicus*. The round-headed saloon doorcases at Blenheim, designed in 1712, are derived from Jones's in the Queen's House. Hawksmoor's respect for Jones was at least equal to Campbell's and founded on closer and earlier acquaintance with his work.

At Christ Church, therefore, Hawksmoor was not merely quoting a leading motif of the new taste; nor was he constructing an enormous frivolity based on it. The whole west front is built up from round and half-round forms in a manner consistent with – and developed from – the other elevations of the church. The side elevations give at first sight that impression common in Hawksmoor buildings of being totally unlike any other building, but their uniqueness is one of combination. The portholes that were intended to light the upper gallery come from Blenheim, ultimately from Hugh May. The round-headed windows breaking across an otherwise continuous impost moulding are most closely paralleled in the elevations of St George-in-the-East, which were conceived at exactly the same date. Nevertheless they are treated differently at Spitalfields, being set in relieving arches; these may be derived from a plate in Palladio, but Hawksmoor extends them downwards to include also the lower windows that lit the aisles under the side galleries. (When the galleries were removed

Ill. 147

Ill. 134

these windows were blocked and the upper ones lengthened.) *Ill. 116* The device of including two tiers of windows in one vertical recess recurs at St Mary Woolnoth; at Spitalfields it is also a means of enriching the relief interest of the wall surface.

A superficial resemblance, on the basis of the portholes, to the sides of Alberti's San Francesco at Rimini has often been noticed. While it is possible, but not demonstrated, that Hawksmoor knew of this building, the rhythm of the openings is exactly opposite in the two cases, for at Rimini the portholes come between and not above the arches. The undeniable

147 Christ Church, Spitalfields. South side

similarity of feeling between the two buildings seems best explained by the fact that Alberti was the first architect of the Renaissance to understand the monumental scale of Roman arcaded structures, while Hawksmoor came nearer than any other Englishman to re-creating it – even though he never saw the originals.

Paradoxically, the interior of Christ Church is distinguished from its companions by the lightness of arcades carried on Composite columns – the slenderest and most ornate of the classical orders. Moreover, it is much more appreciably a long

Ill. 135

Ill. 148 church and not a centrally planned one. The early drawings show no side entrances, and no east and west screens of columns. Nor do they show the intermediate piers, whose introduction had two results: they mark off a central rectangle, and the use of half-columns attached to the piers makes the span of the lateral arches smaller than the centre ones. Thus the design developed from a longitudinal columnar church, nearer the strict form of the basilica than was the 'Primitive Christians' plan (and perhaps consciously so), towards an interior still columnar but planned about two axes. The original seating arrangement conformed to this reading of the interior, having a broad cross aisle between the side doorways; the side galleries (removed in 1866) must have been less at variance with the centralized impression than in the other churches, since the greater number of uprights in the length of the interior made them harder to see.

The loss of the galleries, the side entrances and the steeple ornaments and the lowering of the side windows have damaged Christ Church irreparably; nevertheless it remains as compelling a masterpiece as any of the churches. It is full of surprises – not least when one passes the west front and finds the great *Ill. 149* cavities hollowed out of the massive front of the belfry stage. Among the 'mere Gothique heaps of stone, without form or order' as the Palladian critic James Ralph called the churches in 1734, this was the one he selected for 'the severest condemnation'. It has more of the 'Solemn & Awfull Appearance' demanded by Vanbrugh than any of the others, and it is hardly

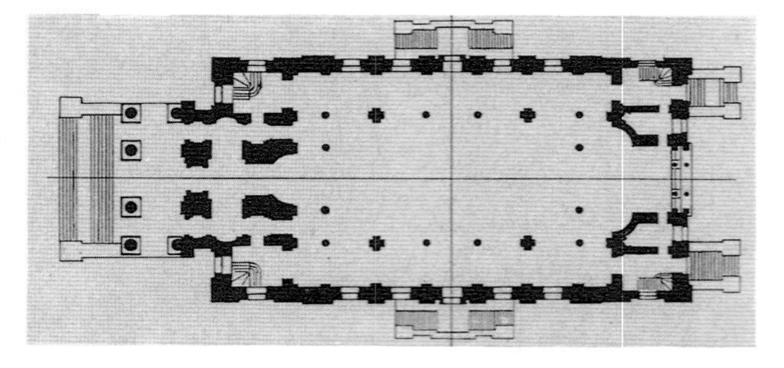

148 Christ Church. Plan

149 Christ Church. Steeple

surprising that the great age of Taste could make little of it. The twentieth century has paid hardly more than lip service to it, but it is to be hoped that never again will it be in danger of demolition as a neglected structure, a redundant church and the wrong category of monument to qualify for state aid.

'Mr Rafe the Critick' was taken to task by Hawksmoor for his 'use of the word Gothick to signifye every thing that displeases him, as the Greeks and Romans calld every Nation Barbarous that, were not in their way of Police and Education'. Hawksmoor's letters to the Dean of Westminster make it clear that for him Gothic was a stylistic term, but one that included Romanesque as well as architecture with pointed arches. In justifying to the Dean his design for the west towers of the Abbey he claimed considerable knowledge of English medieval architecture. In 1716–20 he supervised repairs and embellishments to Beverley Minster, including the addition of a 'Gothick' choir screen, nave galleries on Doric pillars and a Corinthian baldacchino (all since destroyed) and probably the wooden ceiling flower over the crossing and the carved inner west doors, which survive. In 1716 he published an engraving with an appeal for funds, and in 1721 he prepared a similar print of St Alban's Abbey to 'Support this venerable pile from being Martyr'd by ye Neglect of a Slouthfull generation'. His interest in Gothic forms goes back to the Warwick design in the 1690s, but it was in 1715 at All Souls, Oxford, that he became most seriously concerned at one and the same time with the design of new 'Gothick' buildings and with the preservation of medieval ones.

Ill. 150

The earliest attempt to add pseudo-medieval buildings to All Souls was probably a scheme of 1708 for a new hall by John Talman, the son of William and first Secretary of the Society of Antiquaries; his design is heavily overlaid with heraldry and with crockets. Hawksmoor's 1709 sketch for a High Street front, illusionist rather than scholarly, entailed doubling the length of the existing street front. By the beginning of 1714 the College had decided to build the library, for

Ill. 68

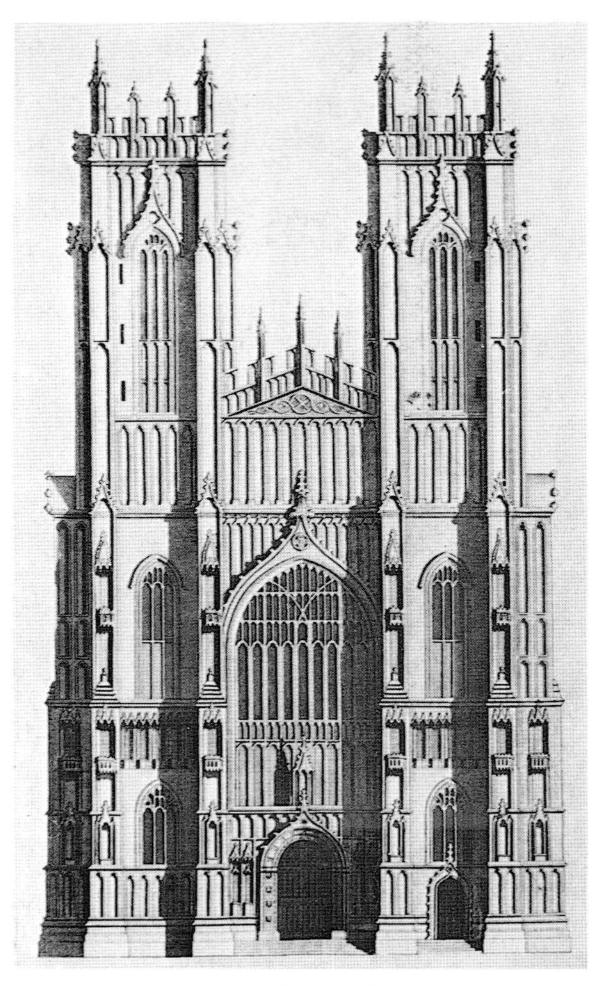

150 Hawksmoor's plate of Beverley Minster

which the Codrington legacy of 1710 (p. 76) made provision, on the site at the north of All Souls; a year later Hawksmoor sent Clarke a number of large drawings for a scheme with the north library, lodgings with twin towers on the east, a 'cloister' on the west, and a remodelling rather than a rebuilding of the southern half of the site. The whole scheme is in 'Gothick' and was accompanied by an extremely long letter or *Explanation* dated 17 February 1715. This makes it clear that, although he included two sketches 'of Rebuilding after ye Antique keeping ye Hall & Chapell Gothick only' he was enthusiastic about the idea of a Gothick All Souls, whoever had suggested it. It also shows that he had abandoned the idea of a complete rebuilding except as a remote possibility, for he pleaded for the preservation of whatever was good in the old work: 'What ever is good in its kinde ought to be preserv'd in respect for antiquity, as well as our present advantage, for destruction can be profitable to none but such as live by it.' Nevertheless it is open to doubt how far his arguments were aesthetic or antiquarian. His plea was that sound masonry, though old, is better and more valuable than shabby new work. 'Preservation' is a relative term, and Hawksmoor was 'confident that much conveniency and beauty may be added' to the old work by such means as 'putting in some Windows carefully or perhaps enlarging others, as necessity may require'. He also 'added upon paper an Upper Storey in form of a perpetuall Arcade of ye Gothick manner that may be open or sollid as apt as needfull, and . . . preserve a Reasonable uniformity'. One of the practical virtues of the whole design of 1715 was that it could be built in two halves; the southern half was never touched, but sketches and the engravings of his designs issued in 1717 and 1721 show that the 'reasonable uniformity' remained in his mind.

Ill. 151

151 Project for street front, All Souls, 1721

152 St Michael, Cornhill. Tower

Work began in 1716 with the library and the centre part and south tower of the east range; the rest of the east range had to wait for further benefactions in 1720 and 1724. The cloister was not begun until 1728, the hall and buttery on the south not till 1730. By extraordinary good fortune the design was followed for the whole exterior in general terms and for some details with great exactness: as late as 1734 William King contracted to finish the battlements between the towers according to the 'printed drawing'.

Hawksmoor did not think like a medieval architect: he did not understand – or perhaps worry about – the linear energy of Gothic architecture. The detail of the north quadrangle is minimally Gothic and includes pure Romanesque corbel tables; his tower of St Michael, Cornhill (1718–24) has similar ones and succeeds in suggesting a Gothic tower without using any pointed arches! The common-room front between the towers

Ill. 152

Ill. 156 at All Souls has a scarcely disguised Venetian window. On the other hand, he urges at length in the Explanation that the windows should be recessed as deeply as possible in the wall 'because ye Wooden Works is defended from ye rain and more Strongly fix'd, besides ye beauty it gives the Overture by Receding'. In medieval architecture he appreciated and strove to imitate the bold and massive but unclassical strength of

Romanesque, and the capacity for holding light and shadow of Gothic. On a sunny day All Souls offers a re-creation of the chiaroscuro pattern of Gothic buildings. The towers have a fairy-tale character. From a distance they seem small and delicate, but within the quadrangle (which always looks too spacious in photographs) they are huge and as dominant as their classical contemporary at Limehouse. *Ill. 109*

154 Oxford. All Souls. Library. Reconstruction of projected ceiling, not executed

◀ 153 All Souls. Catte Street front

155 All Souls. Hawksmoor's plan (redrawn): (a) Gateway and Cloister (not built), (b) Chapel, (c) Hall, (d) Buttery (e) Cloister. (f) Library as planned

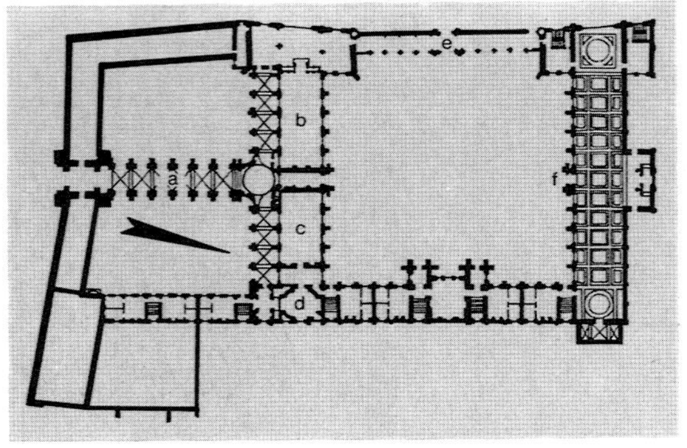

156 Oxford. All Souls. North quadrangle from south-west

The library, although it was not fitted up either in Hawksmoor's life-time or according to his intentions, is still a fine building; with some imagination it can be seen as he wanted it. The principal entrance is in the centre, as in the gallery at Easton Neston or the Kensington Orangery; the door should have opened dramatically to face a large aedicule or niche in the centre recess, and to reveal the full extent of the interior to left and right. Older libraries were usually upstairs and could only be entered from the end; moreover, they were usually lit from both sides and arranged with seats and desks, separated by bookstacks, running from the side walls to a centre gangway. Hawksmoor arranged the bookshelves along the walls, with a narrow gallery along the windowless north side. The ceiling which he designed but which was never carried out would have defined the interior in a way the present one cannot do: the end compartments had roundels in squares and the rest was coffered with a square and two smaller rectangles to each bay. *Ill. 154*

The All Souls interiors are also surprising because they are classical, not Gothick. A certain amount of paraphrase and masking even accommodates the end Venetian windows to the tracery of the library exterior. *Ill. 153* The common room has a kind of very shallow rib vault which owes something to Gothic profiles. The hall and buttery are altogether more remarkable. The oval buttery is vaulted with carved coffered stones, a few years earlier than the similar stones of the saucer dome of the Mausoleum. *Ills. 157, 181* The hall is rectangular in plan, but has a plaster vault wrapped over the interior like the inside of a great balloon. *Ill. 158* No other roof in England shows such free plasticity which is closer to certain rooms by Borromini or the church vaults of Central European Baroque, none of which Hawksmoor is likely to have known. Sketches suggest that the end walls and the panelling owe a good deal to Clarke and Townesend; but the form of the vault must be Hawksmoor's, and the screen, which curves upwards in a contrary configuration to that of the vault, appears in one of his 1717 engravings.

Hawksmoor's extraordinary fecundity of invention was very

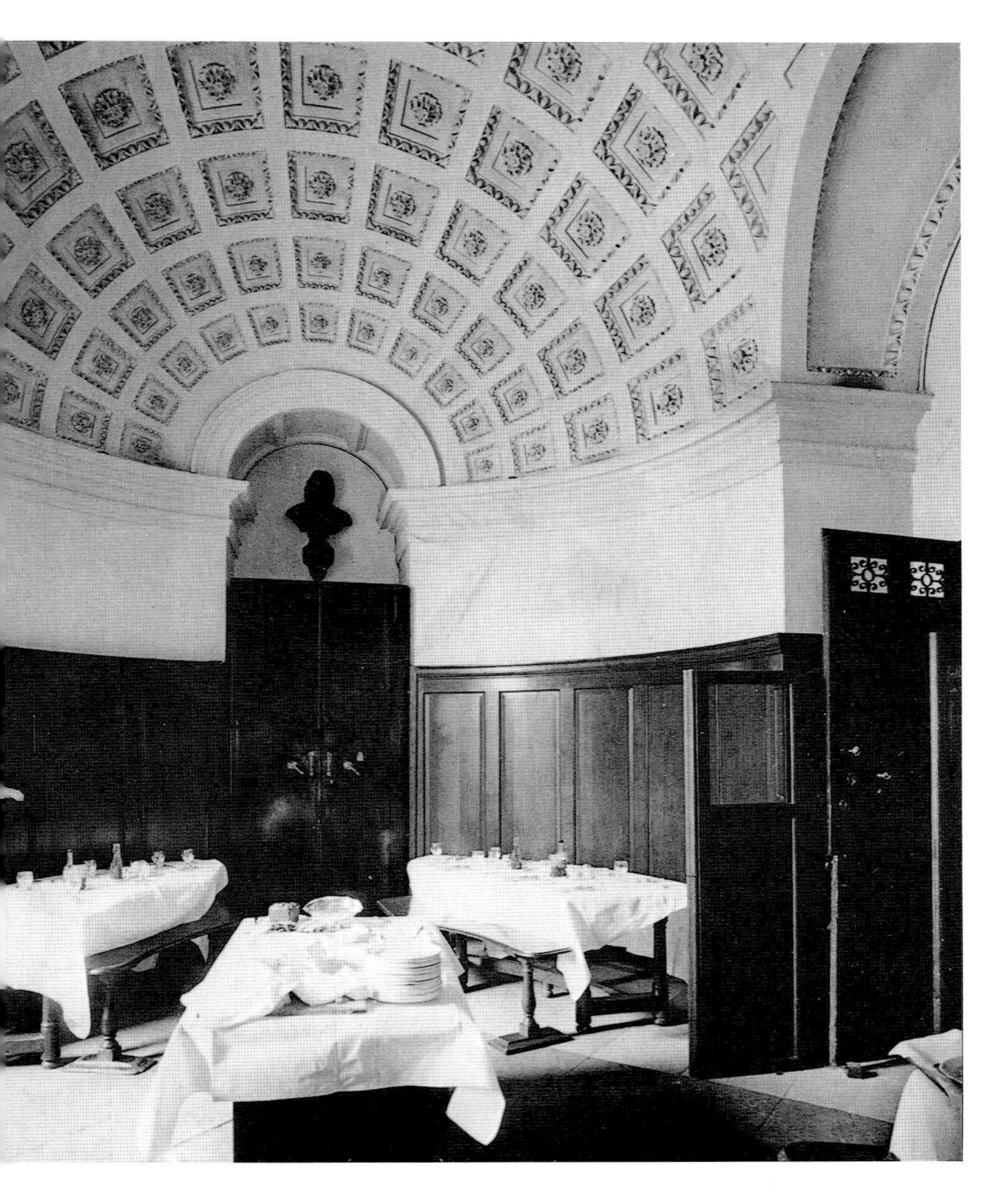

157 All Souls. Buttery

largely lost on Oxford and Cambridge. This was not simply the result of the expensiveness of his imaginative schemes, or even of the limited architectural vision of the majority of eighteenth-century dons. There was an element of the cosy and the picturesque in the buildings of our senior universities even when they were new; the two great colleges that prove the rule are not even exceptions to it, for Christ Church, Oxford and King's College, Cambridge were left unfinished. Hawksmoor's idea of a college did not include crooked little passages leading to irregular courts and isolated blocks, features that for him were too much like those resurrected after the Great Fire of London instead of 'a convenient regular well built Citty' and which he attacked in the *Explanation.* The effect of his heroic porticoes, colonnades and towers could fairly be called explosive; in the hands of a lesser artist it could well be overpoweringly dull. All Souls succeeds in being neither. It is gentle and quiet and not quite credible, and the interiors almost persuade us that academic life would have been possible – and fruitful – inside the other brave designs. All Souls, rather than the Mausoleum, is his own monument, and it is both appropriate and easy to feel there the warmer side of his character.

158 All Souls, The hall

CHAPTER SEVEN

Wisdom

Of the extant letters of Hawksmoor 103, nearly two thirds, date from between 1722 and 1736; 76 of these are at Castle Howard and were written to Lord Carlisle concerning either the works there or Hawksmoor's attempts to regain his stature in the Office of Works through Carlisle's interest. This pattern of survival is unlikely to be entirely accidental, for the journey from London to Yorkshire was a formidable one and the architect's health was variable. He made it at least once in his later years, in 1731, but that was probably the last time he saw the buildings there. Their progress otherwise depended on correspondence and the capacity of William Etty on the spot to understand and interpret his instructions. Etty's death in July 1734 was a considerable blow; Doe, the mason from Studley Royal who succeeded as Clerk of Works, appeared to him competent enough but never established the *rapport* Hawksmoor had enjoyed with Etty. Some of the letters contain only the 'sundry instructions usefull for the Workmen' for which Hawksmoor wished his patron to keep them, but others were written with a further purpose. Carlisle was under attack from Whigs younger than himself, including Sir Thomas Robinson, an amateur architect who became his son-in-law in 1728; his continued support of Vanbrugh and Hawksmoor was out of step with the march of Taste. He may have felt on occasion that chapter and verse would be useful buttresses to a confidence founded on his personal loyalty to his architects; Hawksmoor certainly thought so, even before Vanbrugh's death in 1726 left him as sole architect. He 'wou'd not mention Authors and Antiquity, but that we have so many conceited Gentlemen full of this science, ready to knock you down, unless you have some old father to stand by you'. Hawksmoor's

159 Castle Howard. The Mausoleum

range of authorities was impressive, but it is clear from the letters and buildings that for him practical considerations were more important than academic rules. This was the basis of his 'theory of architecture' and as a result we have to piece it together from isolated and incidental statements made in particular circumstances.

The work of Hawksmoor's last fifteen years is less even in quality. In the case of the last two churches, for which documents show him to have been at least partly responsible, the circumstances of the work account for a good deal. Most of the unsuccessful competition designs for St Giles-in-the-Fields look as if his heart was not in them. He probably drew rather less: the project for Magdalen College of 1724 is 'but a Scizza' – a couple of rough sketches – and the number of dictated letters as well as some rather shaky or inelegant but indubitably autograph drawings testify to the effect of his ailment. A note on a sketch for one of the drawings he sent to Yorkshire tells its own tale: *Gout – Gout. Belvidera at Castle Howard Dec 1723. Gout.* Possibly in later years he needed not less but more time to think and room to manipulate. Certainly there is nothing second-rate about the Long Library or the Woodstock Arch at Blenheim, the Westminster towers or the Mausoleum.

Between 1716 and 1722 Hawksmoor had no part in the continuation of Blenheim; there is a sketch dated 1720, for a garden bridge, but in the following year the Duchess of Marlborough included him in the 401 persons accused in her lawsuit of conspiring 'to load the Duke of Marlborough with ye payment of the debts due on account of ye Building'. Perhaps she could hardly have made an exception of him in so monstrous a suit. Vanbrugh was never allowed in the grounds after 1716 though he once managed to look over a wall. But in April 1722 Hawksmoor wrote to the Duchess: 'Your Grace, I am inform'd, is finishing the Bridge and other affairs, which I most extreamly commend and applaud.' There is a good deal of flattery in the letter, together with the offer 'to serve you, in the best manner I am able, if my advice can be any ways

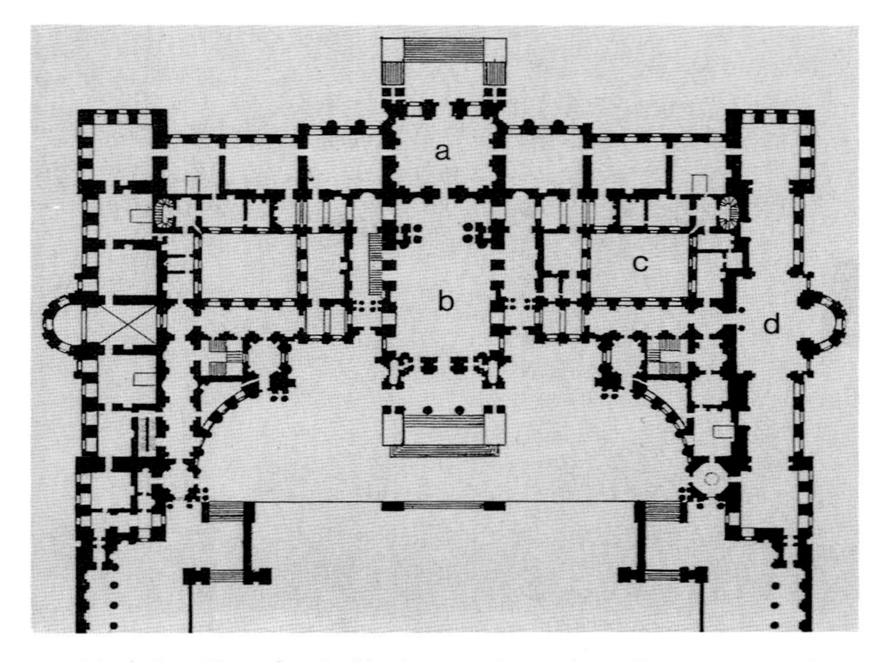

160 Blenheim. Plan of main block: (a) Saloon, (b) Hall, (c) Courtyard, (d) Library

usefull, of this Affair your Grace is a very good judge'. Letters and drawings show that works which perhaps exceeded the capacity of the oracular Moore (p. 63) and of John Desborough as Clerk of Works were now entrusted to Hawksmoor, and he made several visits to Blenheim. *Ill. 160*

The ceilings in three rooms in the east half of the south side were designed by him; their novel form is marred by later heavy gilding and the neo-Rococo ornament added in the corners; the latter blurs the distinction which the architect had preserved in the combination of two traditional types of ceiling. The heavy fret seems to hang in space; not however from a flat ceiling but from a deeply coved one of the kind usually intended for illusionist painting. This combination is foreshadowed in St Alfege, Greenwich but the effect of suspension against gravity is more remarkable within the confines of the Blenheim rooms. *Ill. 161*

161 Blenheim. Ceiling of Green Writing Room

Ill. 165 With the Long Library Hawksmoor had the task of making a room out of the shell left by Vanbrugh for the gallery that Marlborough had wanted from the start. Its basic shape was settled very early, but it is marked on a plan of 1716 as not ceiled and only partly roofed. When Hawksmoor wrote the Duchess had already decided on its completion, and he was much concerned that it 'will be a room of distinguished Beauty if rightly managed and on the other hand, it may suffer much, if it is not finished with Skill'. He succeeded in providing designs for the fine plasterwork of Isaac Mansfield, the marble *Ill. 162* pilasters and doorcase of William Townesend and Bartholomew Peisley and the carved bookcases of which only fragments survive in the casework of the organ installed in 1891. This

162 Blenheim. Long Library doorcase

163 Blenheim. Long Library. South dome

164 Blenheim. Long Library. Intermediate ceiling

remarkable room, 180 feet long, has a chequered history. It was converted from its intended function by the addition of bookcases after the Duchess's acquisition of the library of her son-in-law the third Earl of Sunderland, who died in 1722. The lower windows in the end sections under the towers were then blocked on the inside by the bookcases, but it is still possible to see from the outside that the window reveals had already been finished with honeycomb coffering like the rest. In 1881–2 the seventh Duke sold the Sunderland library and part of the proceeds was used to reconvert the room to its original purpose as a picture gallery; ironically the eighth Duke sold the great collection of old masters in 1885. Under the ninth Duke's programme of restoration new pastiche bookcases were made and restocked with books, and apart from the organ (now at the north end) the room is in spirit much as Hawksmoor left it.

165 Blenheim. Long Library from north

The Long Library is the last of the long narrow Hawksmoor rooms such as the gallery at Easton Neston and the library at All Souls, but it is quite different from them in plan and in treatment. One pilaster-articulation and a common type of decoration are applied to the whole room, but at the same time Hawksmoor accepted, and emphasized, the implication of the plan: that it consists of five distinct sections. They are of different widths, and he made them of different heights. He raised plaster domes into the end towers – sections to which he referred as 'Salon in ye Gallery' or 'ye Cabinet of ye Gallery' in recognition of their spatial independence. In the three middle sections height and width are related, and there are no lines or planes continuous from one section to the next. The Duchess decided before its completion to dispense with the decorative painting originally planned. The Long Library is no richer than the hall and saloon and less ostentatious, and architecturally the finest room at Blenheim; this is due partly to Hawksmoor's superb control of detail and partly to his treatment of the room as a sequence of related spaces which are interesting whether entered from the middle or from either end.

Ill. 163

The Duchess considered the outworks that seemed to spring from the earth around Vanbrugh houses a colossal waste of money. Vanbrugh's bridge (it was really a viaduct until Capability Brown dammed the stream into a lake under it) she had always thought 'ridiculous' as well as extravagant, but she decided to make it at least usable. And when the Duke died in June 1722 and left her '£10,000 a year to Spoil Blenheim her own way' as Vanbrugh put it, she had the means as well as the wish to make the palace a personal monument to her hero. Hawksmoor had already suggested 'some proper Inscription to show the Succeeding Ages to whom, they were obliged for defending their Liberties'. The bridge is on the axial approach to the palace, but nobody ever comes that way down the two-mile avenue. Sightseers have always come through Woodstock, and the gate towards the town seemed the obvious place for an inscription. In November Hawksmoor, who had had

166 Blenheim. Woodstock gate

such a structure in mind for a couple of years, gave Peisley the designs for the Triumphal Arch, including 'the Moldings & Cornices'. He also drew out the letters for the Latin inscription on the outer face of the attic; the face towards the park has an English translation. The Woodstock Gate is so restrained and classical in feeling that, in spite of the date 1723 in the inscriptions, it was once attributed to Sir William Chambers who added various embellishments to Blenheim in the 1760s. It

Ill. 166

suggests a work of Imperial Rome, though there seems to be no Roman prototype for an arch of this kind having an attic of less than the full width of the structure. There is a curious misrepresentation of the Arch of Titus in this form in several pictures by Claude, and Hawksmoor possibly knew one of these, or he may have reached the form from his own invention. The 'Roman' feeling of the gate and the location of its source are of some importance because Hawksmoor, whose mind often worked by association of certain ideas with certain types of building, seems to have been particularly aware of the iconography of commemorative structures. Moreover, in his later years he seems to have been especially interested in such associations, although probably less for their funerary nature than in relation to a kind of creative archaeology. The steeple of St George, Bloomsbury, is very far from an 'exact' reconstruction of the Tomb of Mausolus as it is known from written sources, but at one stage in the design of St Mary Woolnoth he seems to have had in mind the Egyptian Hall of Vitruvius and Palladio, and a project for Brasenose College, Oxford is based on Palladio's idea of a Roman house. In this context the late park buildings at Castle Howard assume an added meaning; so too does Hawksmoor's concern with columns and obelisks.

Ill. 167

The 'historical pillar' in Blenheim Park was finally set up in 1727–31 to the design of Lord Herbert, amateur architect, later ninth Earl of Pembroke. Hawksmoor saw it in October 1731 and called on the Duchess 'to trye what she wou'd doe' as he told Lord Carlisle, 'but hir Grace . . . was not so Gratious as to see me'; this is the only comment we have on the architect's final dissociation from Blenheim. But the idea of an obelisk at Blenheim goes back to 1714–15; its inspiration then was the obelisk raised in 1714 at Castle Howard in honour of Marlborough, but at Blenheim the Duke and Vanbrugh seem to have had in mind the romantic associations of Woodstock with Henry II and Fair Rosamond – to the disgust of the Duchess. Ten years later she had accepted the place of a

167 Henry Herbert, 9th Earl of Pembroke. Blenheim. The Column

monumental pillar in the new idea of Blenheim as a personal memorial, and Hawksmoor sent a number of drawings for columns and obelisks, with a written *Explanation of the Obelisk*, describing his designs and discussing possible sites. This document shows that he intended the visitor's approach to Blenheim to be both a didactic and a spatial experience.

Ill. 168

The Woodstock Gate is so placed that it cannot be seen until the visitor enters the little square at the end of the street in which it is set. Pausing to read the inscription he learns (as the *Explanation* puts it) 'that the (Reader) or Traveler will know more by the Column (or Obelisk) Set up at ye Entrance'; thus the pillar, Hawksmoor says, 'should not be placed out of Sight, or at a Mile Distance'. Although he considered several positions, these remarks presuppose that it should be placed between the Woodstock Gate and the house at the point where the road bends round to the right. Thus it should advertise the position of the palace and mark the change of direction; by architectural means the spectator's movements would be controlled within the surroundings of the palace. Moreover, the inscription on the pillar, in conjunction with that on the Gate, should instruct the visitor in the meaning and purpose of the buildings to which he was thus directed. This scheme is the successor, on a smaller scale and with a very specific intention, of the environmental plans of the preceding decade. The column in its final position is a more picturesque object but a far less meaningful one, and the inscription on the Gate remains for ever to show that it is in the wrong place.

Hawksmoor's sketches include one for a column, showing that the change from an obelisk was not due to the invention of Lord Herbert; indeed Hawksmoor seems to have had in mind his own design of 1714 for a column in honour of Queen Anne, and it is also interesting if not significant that in 1723 he drew for engraving Wren's design for the Monument to the Great Fire with a figure of Charles II on the top.

The obelisk drawings are unusual – and peculiar to their designer – in having extremely big pedestals, a form of support that by tradition belongs to a column such as that of Marcus Aurelius in Rome or Wren's Fire Monument. It was in 1724 that he wrote to Lord Carlisle about some small obelisks for Castle Howard that 'I woud not let them stand upon ye cold ground' and enclosed a sketch for a similar high base. Historical correctness took second place to Hawksmoor's conception of the pillar as a separate and exotic object to be placed on a pedestal like a statue.

Ill. 168

168 Project for the Blenheim memorial

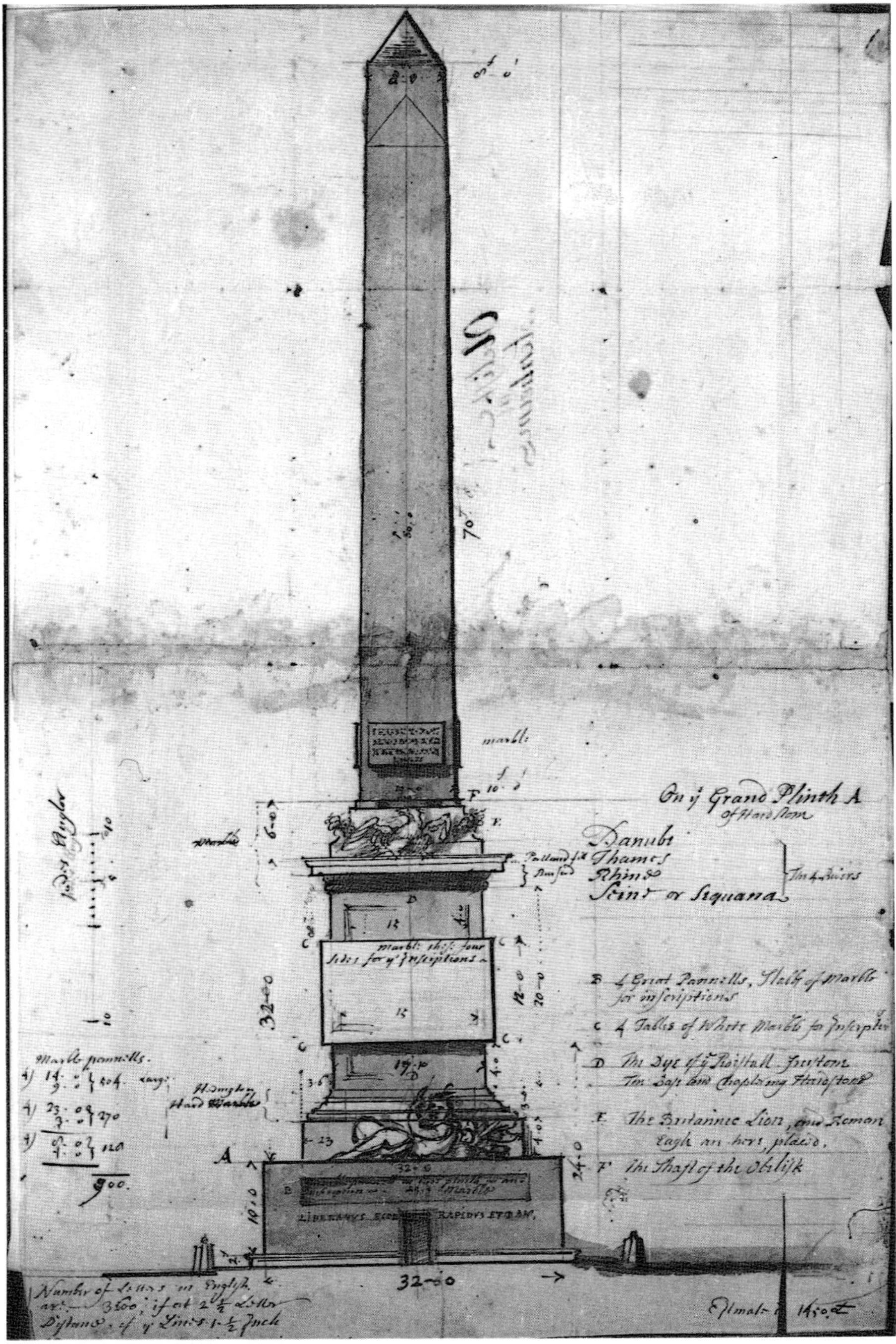

On ye Grand Plinth A of Hardston

Danube
Thames
Rhine
Seine or Sequana

The 4 Rivers

marble

Portland stone

marble these four sides for ye Inscriptions

B 4 Great Pannells, Stelt of Marble for inscriptions

C 4 Tables of White Marble for Inscription

D The Dye of ye Roistall Freeston
The Base and Chapiterg Hardstone

E The Britannic Lion, and Roman Eagle as here placed.

F The Shaft of the Obilisk

Marble pannells.
4) 14.0 / 9.0 } 504
4) 23.0 / 3.0 } 270
4) 5.0 / 9.0 } 120
900.

Hard Marble

LIBERAVUS ECCE ... RAPIDUS ET DAN.

32-0 ... 24-0 ... 10-0 ... 32-00 ... 70-0 ... 12-0 ... 20-0 ... 6-0

Number of Letters in English are 3500, if at 2½ Letter Distance of ye Lines 1½ Inch

Estimate 1450£

The Duchess's decision not to retain Hawksmoor came at about the same time as the agreement of the Fifty New Churches Commission to start two further churches, on sites at Old Street and Horselydown, north of the City and in Bermondsey respectively. On 5 May 1727 Hawksmoor and James were asked as Surveyors to prepare a design and estimate for a church

170 Hawksmoor and John James. St John, Horselydown

169 Hawksmoor and John James. St Luke, Old Street

to cost, with the parsonage and churchyard enclosure, not more than the prescribed £10,000; this measure reflected the fact that the earlier churches had been far more costly; St George-in-the-East, for example, had cost over £26,000. Five weeks later, when designs were produced, the Surveyors were ordered to prepare jointly a design to be built as cheaply as possible; after a further two weeks plans for the two specific sites were approved and work was put in hand. This sequence of events looks very much like a stratagem by the Commissioners to tie their architects to a fixed price and design; they were interested in churches as necessities and not as monuments of art or ideology, and it seems probable that the peculiarities of St Luke, Old Street and St John, Horselydown, were due to their joint authorship and to the fact that Hawksmoor, to whom second thoughts were important, was not allowed to change his mind about the designs. Both churches have suffered in the twentieth century: St Luke became dangerous through war damage and neglect, but the obelisk steeple survives as a landmark. St John was bombed and the steeple taken down. Both were simple nave-and-aisles churches of a plainness of which James might be proud but which lacks the vigour of other plain Hawksmoor exteriors. Their steeples, splendid but bizarre advertisements of their presence, were by no means without parallel in Hawksmoor's work. In 1714 he drew a steeple for St Anne, Limehouse, with an Ionic capital as its finial; later he put Roman altars on St George-in-the-East and a stepped pyramid on the tower at Bloomsbury, and in 1730 he drew obelisk-steeples for St Giles-in-the-Fields. The fluted obelisk and tapering Ionic column belong, in 1727–30, in the sequence of these objects; like the others, they are architectural forms complete in themselves but elevated from 'the cold ground' to the skyline in an unfamiliar context.

Ill. 169

Ill. 170

Ill. 171

The garden works at Castle Howard also include, among those remote from the house, a small rusticated pyramid set on a high base, and an object on a similar base known as the 'Four Faces'. Such monuments are usually associated with the

1 Project for steeple, Giles-in-the-Fields

172 Castle Howard. The Four Faces

four seasons and with roads crossing at right angles; this one stands at what seems always to have been an informal intersection. It consists of a four-faced urn pinnacle similar to – and perhaps left over from – those on the parapet of the great house, and thus appears to anticipate the 'ready-mades' of the twentieth century. It is clear from documents that there were originally more pedestals and objects at Castle Howard than there are today.

Ill. 172

The unique landscape of this place, which in spite of decimation by time and the elements still seems peopled with monuments, was the joint creation of Vanbrugh, Hawksmoor and Carlisle, and it is doubtful whether it will ever be possible to separate their shares. A poem entitled *Castle Howard*, published in London and probably written by Carlisle's daughter Anne, Viscountess Irwin about 1733, treats him as the author of the idea of the landscape, and the letters of the architects show not only his interest in every stage but the extent to which they engaged his collaboration. This is especially relevant to the two most important buildings after the house itself: Vanbrugh's Temple and Hawksmoor's Mausoleum. Both were finished posthumously, the last works of their designers. It is certain that the Temple, begun in 1726, was carried out faithfully by Hawksmoor, whose own intentions for a building on that site were quite different: early in 1724 he had described Vanbrugh's design in a letter, contrasting it with his own. The interior of the Temple was the work of neither architect but of the Italian stuccoist Vassali and was not carried out until 1737–9. The Mausoleum, to replace as a family vault the old Henderskelfe church which had been demolished to make way for the house, was under discussion in 1726 but was not begun until three years later. The attic and dome were built soon after 1736, still in accordance with Hawksmoor's intentions, but the outer surrounding wall and the big flight of steps up to the entrance are the work of a minor Palladian, Daniel Garrett, and contradict Hawksmoor's ideas.

Ill. 174

Ill. 159

The poem describes how

> Buildings the proper Points of View adorn,
> Of *Grecian*, *Roman* and *Egyptian* Form

and the author's footnote identifies these as 'The Obelisk, Temple, Mausoleum, and Pyramid', without saying which is which. The Obelisk of 1714 in honour of Marlborough and the big Pyramid of 1728 which is a monument to Lord William Howard, the Elizabethan founder of the estate, are obviously

Ill. 173

173 Castle Howard. The Pyramid

of Egyptian form but it is not easy to find a specifically Greek or Roman character in the other two buildings. The difficulty lies partly in the nebulous ideas of Greek architecture entertained in western Europe before the middle of the century, but these ideas themselves add to the significance of the poet's identification. The buildings were conceived as examples of the three greatest historical styles of Antiquity. This conception reflects an interest in ancient exemplars, parallel and contemporary with the publication of Fischer von Erlach's *Entwurff einer historischen Architektur* in 1721; an interest that is very marked in Hawksmoor, as has already been shown, and which he seems to have derived at some time from Wren.

Ill. 174 Vanbrugh's Temple, which stands at the opposite end of the same spine of high ground as the house, is, like Campbell's Mereworth and Lord Burlington's Chiswick Villa (both built in the 1720s), based on Palladio's Villa Rotonda, a square house with a central domed hall and four identical porticoes. It is a far less literal derivation, being smaller, a single-roomed summer-house, and having far more height in proportion to ground area. In its tallness and in the prismatic simplicity of its central cube, its hemispherical dome and deep porticoes it is paradoxically more Italian in feeling than the more doctrinaire neo-Palladian villas; unlike them it could easily have come from the Roman Campagna or from a Claude landscape, and its presence imbues the Yorkshire scenery with an extraordinary Virgilian quality. This is perhaps an indication that the Temple represented for the poet of Castle Howard the Roman form.

174 Vanbrugh. Castle Howard. The Temple

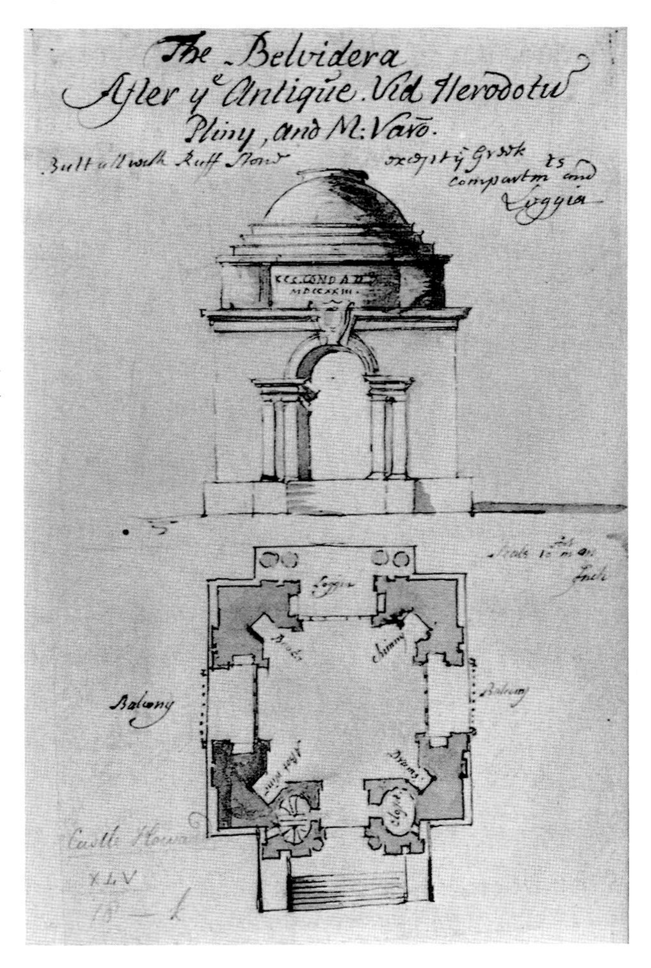

175 First project for a belvedere at Castle Howard

Hawksmoor had put forward and described in his letter two ideas for a Belvedere of 'common Wall stone' as an alternative to the Temple. One was square in plan with a dome; he gave as source for the 'figure' or general elevation Vignola's little church of Sant' Andrea on the Flaminian Way north-west of Rome. He did not mention that his model was rectangular with an oval dome; he may have known this and considered it

Ill. 175

176 Second project for a belvedere at Castle Howard

irrelevant, or he may have been misled by Falda's engraved view in which this peculiarity is not evident. The sketch is specifically entitled 'The Belvidera After ye Antique' with an inscrutable reference to Herodotus, Pliny and Varro. It may be significant that the English edition of Montfaucon's *L'antiquité expliquée* appeared in 1722: the sections on the Ancients' country houses in Vol. III include the Younger Pliny's villa at

Laurentinum and 'a singular parlour for eating' belonging to Varro, as well as several references to Herodotus. Montfaucon would therefore offer a convenient single source for a rather pedantic allusion to the Belvedere as a place to eat and drink, read and contemplate.

The only other clue to the design's significance for Hawksmoor is the description in the letter of the 'apertures' as 'ornaments after ye Greek manner', a description that raises rather than solves problems. The doorway is an arch resting on pilaster imposts and belongs to the same family as his adumbrations of the Venetian window (p. 153). Even without the insistence of the poem that the garden contained a Greek form, it is desirable to inquire what *Greek* meant for Hawksmoor. The second design for the Belvedere, a concave-sided octagon that seems obviously indebted to Borromini, may have an Antique prototype in the little polygonal Temple of Venus at Baalbek. The third (1714) and later editions of Dr Maundrell's posthumously published *Journey from Aleppo to Jerusalem* have plates signed by Hawksmoor of the Temple of Jupiter at Baalbek, based on plates by Jean Marot. But Hawksmoor also knew Maundrell's successor as Chaplain to the Levant Company, Dr Lisle, and gathered information about Baalbek from him, and as the polygonal temple was in use as a church Lisle is quite likely to have described it to him. It may be relevant that Marot calls Baalbek 'en Grèce'. It was not universally clear in Hawksmoor's time that ancient Greek construction relied totally on beams without making use of the arch; moreover, it was still possible to apply the term *Greek*, as Vasari had done, to Byzantine art, thus including the whole of eastern Mediterranean art of the early post-Classical period. In 1714–15 Hawksmoor contrasted Greek *or* Antique (he used both words) and Gothick designs for All Souls (p. 199) on a single sheet which he then cut into two. *Greek* may have been no more precise for him than, on the one hand, 'non-Roman Antique', and on the other, 'using columns instead of piers to carry arches'; the latter is perhaps most familiar to us through

Ill. 176

Ill. 177

the nineteenth-century revival of Italian Byzantine and Romanesque forms, but the Venetian window is one example of it with a history traceable back to late Antiquity. There is a parallel ambiguity of terms in Hawksmoor's use of *Gothic* and *monastic* interchangeably and to include Romanesque (p. 160).

It seems possible, then, that the Mausoleum was in some way Greek for Hawksmoor and Carlisle. The latter originally suggested a Greek temple for his family's burial chapel, but the architect was quick to point out that this was inappropriate since 'the Gentiles, Jews, or any other polite people had either Magnificent piles for Sepulture, but never buryed near their temples, or built their tombs in the form of any temple dedicated to divine honours'. Instead he mentioned the Mausoleum of Harlicarnassus (p. 138) and the mysterious Tomb of Porsenna supposedly at Clusium (whose pyramids may have inspired those of the Carrmire Gate at Castle Howard) and the 'many forms of this nature of fabrick the designs of which are published in ye Books of Antiquity, that your Lordship may see at pleasure'. Carlisle and his son and heir Lord Morpeth seem to have taken up this offer, and in July 1728 Hawksmoor sent a design based on the Tomb of Cecilia Metella on the Appian Way, a large masonry cylinder on a square podium. His design, only known from his covering letter, was crowned with some sort of dome and had clerestory windows invisible from outside. The clerestory seems to have crystallized in his mind a historical sequence of circular buildings associated with death, baptism and eternity – concepts which are mystically related – extending from Antiquity to his own time. Notable relevant examples are Bramante's Tempietto, Wren's 1678 project for a Mausoleum for Charles I, Hawksmoor's own designs for a baptistery for St Paul's and those for the Radcliffe Library, which was a memorial building though not a funerary one. During the autumn of 1728 he developed a design for a domed cylinder rising out of and above a larger lower cylindrical arcade. Many minor changes were still to be made and one major one: before building began in April 1729 the design was

Ill. 185

Ills. 74, 79

177 Alternatives for the west side of All Souls, Greek and Gothick (redrawn)

transformed from an arcaded to a colonnaded one. This had the direct effect of raising the height of the elevation by six feet and the indirect one of producing a post-and-lintel peristyle which Carlisle may have considered Greek rather than Roman. It appears to have been Carlisle's suggestion, but by this time Hawksmoor had offered him so many ideas that he is as likely to have responded to discreet persuasion from his architect. Hawksmoor was thereafter 'entirely for a Colonade' provided that big enough stones could be found to bridge the entablature.

The latitude Hawksmoor appears from the correspondence to have allowed his patron, and the number of changes made even during construction, almost give the impression that he did not know what he wanted and that the final result was a matter of chance. In a case of less evident sympathy between architect and patron this might well be dangerously true, but Hawksmoor's method of 'experience and trials' was a perfectly conscious one (pp. 21, 35). Wren had experimented through most of the building of St Paul's and there are several documented last-minute changes in Hawksmoor's churches. The metaphors he used, of parenthood or midwifery, imply, whether consciously or not, an attitude towards not only a building but also a design as something that develops from birth to maturity. With the Mausoleum he had certainly made up his mind by 1732 when a worried Carlisle relayed to him the scholarly criticism of Lord Burlington that the narrow intercolumniation of a diameter and a half in a Doric circular building had no Antique precedent and was therefore absolutely wrong. The seven pages of justification Hawksmoor then dictated and sent off were largely a smokescreen, but the cogent facts that emerge are that the stone allowed no wider spacing, that Hawksmoor had known this from the start, that building was too far advanced to make any alteration, and that – Antique or not – this was the effect he liked and would not alter 'tho' I should be hired to do it'.

The effect is crowded, as if the columns were a fence to keep the living out and the dead within. In general terms, Hawksmoor was always more concerned with the emotive power of architectural language than with its correctness; the sources he used and named were for him patterns, not doctrinal absolutes. A specific interpretation of the Mausoleum colonnade accords with the meaning of the building: it is the house of the dead, for the *loculi* surrounding the crypt contain the coffins of Carlisle and his family. The Temple, the Pyramid and the Mausoleum all stand, with an apparent casualness that cannot have been accidental, on small hill-tops; they give, as do few other buildings, the impression that we are continually being watched. From near and far off they appear on the skyline where their simple silhouettes are extraordinarily effective. The Mausoleum in particular seems dark and gloomy against the sky and paradoxically lighter inside than without. The outer bastion-wall and Garrett's elaborate staircase are contrary to Hawksmoor's intentions because they extend the building into the landscape and the staircase, modelled on that of Burlington's Chiswick, positively invites us to enter. Hawksmoor designed steps within the podium invisible from the outside (much like the original ascent to St George-in-the-East).

Ill. 182

Ill. 90

178 Castle Howard. The Mausoleum

179 Castle Howard.
The Mausoleum.
Dome

180 Castle Howard.
The Mausoleum.
Interior

181 Castle Howard. The Mausoleum. Dome

The interior has one parallel in architecture more apparent to our eyes than it would have been in Hawksmoor's time, and one he never mentioned: Michelangelo's Medici Chapel. In both buildings the even lighting of the dome – here by a clerestory that can only be seen from the edge of the floor – conceals the exact shape of its surface and makes it seem to float above us. In both cases exit seems harder than entry: the Medici Chapel has eight doorcases and only one door, the Mausoleum has a single door and on the outside three more blind doorcases which were blocked up during construction. In both cases architectural means are employed for an emotional as well as a formal effect; this is not surprising if we consider that Michelangelo prefigured or invented much of the Baroque style of which Hawksmoor was a late and truly English exponent. In the Medici Chapel the normal forms and functions of architectural language are reversed so that, for example, containing shapes do not contain. In the Mausoleum, as a special case of this reversal, the wall appears to press inwards between the columns that articulate the interior; thus the feeling of oppressive enclosure is intensified.

Ill. 179

Ill. 181

In the early 1730s Hawksmoor's designs for All Souls were still under construction (p. 163). In 1733 he gave his final thoughts on the Radcliffe Library and the street front of the Queen's College. The screen wall contains niches of shallow half-oval section, derived from an earlier design of his own for the hall and chapel elevation by way of the niches of St Mary Woolnoth. The delicate cupola containing the statue of Queen Caroline is possibly – but not closely – related to reconstructions of the shrine of Diana at Ephesus. In 1734 he wrote to Dr Clarke with further sketches for Brasenose and Magdalen College. The Surveyorship of Westminster Abbey which he had taken over on Wren's death led to the start of the towers in 1734, and the next year he may have designed the King chapel in Ockham church. He was still worrying about Greenwich Hospital and planning and lobbying for a bridge at Westminster. He seems to have been seriously ill in the winter of

Ill. 78

Ill. 183

182 Castle Howard. The Mausoleum. Crypt passage

1729–30 – not for the first time – and in January he made his will; the tempo of life must have been slowing down.

The world had treated him better materially than morally: he owned several houses but he had been gradually excluded from official architecture and the future lay with the polite and sometimes vacuous refinements of neo-Palladianism. On 2 March 1736, three weeks before his death, a letter in his own hand told Carlisle that he was correcting papers and drawing for Castle Howard and was busy with the Westminster Bridge scheme; he asked for 'recommendations to your friends, that I may be employed in Some Shape or other if I shall be alive in Building the Bridge I have taken so much pains for'. (Charles Labelye's bridge was begun two years later.) His wife survived him for a year. His monument in Shenley churchyard is a plain black slab with a Latin inscription, characteristically erudite: a study of ancient epitaphs suggests that *PMSL* stands for *piae memoriae sacer locus* but the formula appears to be unique. In the last fifty years the previous injustice of history has been repaired by the recognition of his works and a reappraisal of his achievement. His spirit lingers at All Souls. His unostentatious and sympathetic completion of Westminster Abbey gave him enduring though seldom acknowledged popular fame. Yet in terms of architecture the Mausoleum remote on its lonely hill is his greatest achievement. It is one of the last Baroque buildings in the freedom of its sources and the intensity of its direct assault on the emotions. But its geometrical simplicity and its sombre severity look forward to the age of neo-classicism. And the strangeness – even when sources have been analysed – of many of Hawksmoor's formal devices, has found recognition only in the present century's exploration of the subconscious. Ultimately the quality and character of his work cannot be put into prose. Its language is the one he knew best and knew as few other English architects have known: the eloquence of stone.

Ills. 2, 184

183 Oxford. The Queen's College. High Street screen

List of Works

Executed works are distinguished by **bold** *type. A few undated or unidentified projects are omitted.*

Sketch-book, 1683.
Broadfield Hall, Herts. Alterations, *c.* 1690–3. *Destroyed.*
Ingestre, Staffs. Project, 1688.
St Augustine, Watling Street, City. Project for lantern, *c.* 1692.
Christ's Hospital Writing School, City. 1692–5. *Destroyed.*
St Mary, Warwick. Project, *c.* 1694.
Kensington Palace, King's Gallery. 1695–6.
Easton Neston, Northants. ?1695–1710.
St John's College, Cambridge. Proposed bridge, 1698.
Windsor Castle. Project for south front, 1698.
Castle Howard, Yorks. Assisted Vanbrugh, 1699–1726.
Greenwich Hospital, King William Block. South and west ranges, 1699–1707. **Queen Anne Block.** East range, 1700–3.
Hampton Court. Bowling green project, *c.* 1700.
Mausoleum for William III. Project, *c.* 1702.
Greenwich Hospital. Schemes for enlargement. ?1702–11 and later.
?Canterbury Cathedral. Archbishop's throne now at west end. *c.* 1704.
Kensington Palace, Orangery. 1704–5.
Blenheim Palace, Oxon. Assisted Vanbrugh, 1705–16.
The Queen's College, Oxford. Projects, 1708–9.
All Souls College, Oxford. Projects for north and south lodgings, 1708–9.
St Paul's Cathedral. Project for piazza and baptistery, *c.* 1710.
Project for a primitive Christian basilica. 1711–12.
Kensington Charity School. 1711–12. *Destroyed.*
Oxford and Cambridge. Plans for university areas, 1712–13.
King's College, Cambridge. Projects, 1712–13.
Old Clarendon Press, Oxford. 1712–13.
Radcliffe Camera, Oxford. Projects, 1712–15.
St Alfege, Greenwich. 1712–18.
All Saints Church, Oxford. Project for steeple, *c.* 1713–15.
St Anne, Limehouse. 1714–30.
St George-in-the-East, Wapping Stepney. 1714–29.
Christ Church, Spitalfields. 1714–29.

184 London. Westminster Abbey. North-west tower

?St James, Garlickhythe, City. Steeple, 1714–17.
Court of Judicature, Westminster. 1716. *Demolished c.* 1739.
Greenwich Hospital, Queen Anne Block. End loggias, 1716–17.
St George, Bloomsbury. 1716–31.
St Mary Woolnoth, City. 1716–24.
All Souls College, Oxford. North quadrangle, 1716–35.
Beverley Minster, Yorks. Repairs and embellishments, *c.* 1716–20. *Partly destroyed.*
St James's Palace, Stable Yard arcade. 1716–17.
St George the Martyr, Queen Square, alterations, 1717–20. 'Modernized' 1867.
Worcester College, Oxford. Projects, *c.* 1717.
St Michael, Cornhill, City. Steeple, 1718–24.
Jewel Tower, Westminster. Renovations, 1718–19.
Brasenose College, Oxford. Projects, 1720–34.
Colby House, Kensington. *c.* 1720. *Destroyed.*
St Alban's Abbey, Herts. Repairs, *c.* 1722–4.
Blenheim Palace, Oxon. Long Library, south-east rooms, Woodstock gate, 1722–5. Projects for column.
Ockham Park, Surrey. Stables and offices, *c.* 1723–5. *Partly rebuilt.*
Westminster Abbey. Projects for crossing and towers, 1724.
Magdalen College, Oxford. Project, 1724.
St John, Horselydown, Bermondsey. With John James, 1727–33. *Gutted.*
St Luke, Old Street, Finsbury. With John James, 1727–33. *Gutted except steeple.*
Ockham Park, Surrey. Projects, 1727–9.
Westminster Abbey. Choir screen, *c.* 1728. *Destroyed or encased.*
Castle Howard, Yorks. Pyramid, 1728. Mausoleum, 1729–42. Carrmire gate, *c.* 1730. Temple of Venus, 1731–5, *destroyed.*
St Giles-in-the Fields, Bloomsbury. Project, 1730.
The Queen's College, Oxford. Screen to High Street, 1733–6.
Radcliffe Camera, Oxford. Project and model, 1733.
Westminster Abbey. West towers, 1734–45. Gable, 1735.
New Burlington Street, Westminster. House for Anne, Viscountess Irwin, 1735. *Destroyed.*
?Ockham, Surrey. King Chapel. *c.* 1735.
Westminster. Project for approach street and bridge, 1736.

185 Castle Howard. Carrmire gate

Bibliography

A guide to material published up to 1978–9 is to be found (with some unintended duplication) in the standard monograph, K. Downes, *Hawksmoor* (2nd ed., Zwemmer, London, 1979). This also lists Hawksmoor's drawings and letters, and prints some of the latter; the largest published collection of letters is G. Webb, *The letters and drawings . . . relating to the building of the Mausoleum at Castle Howard* (Walpole Society, XIX, 1931).

There have been two Hawksmoor exhibitions in London: in 1962 (Arts Council Gallery; the small catalogue is a collectors' item) and in 1977 (Whitechapel Art Gallery, with a more substantial catalogue).

Serious students will need to use the invaluable but undigested source material in the twenty *Wren Society* volumes (Oxford, 1924–43), and to consult the Vanbrugh volume of *English Homes* (Period IV, ii) by H. A. Tipping and C. Hussey (London, 1928) as well as Geoffrey Webb's edition of Vanbrugh's letters (*The Complete Works of Sir John Vanbrugh*, IV, London, 1928). Hawksmoor's partnership with Vanbrugh remains the subject of controversy, in spite of L. Whistler, *The Imagination of Vanbrugh and his Fellow Artists* (London, 1954), K. Downes, *Vanbrugh* (London, 1977), C. Saumarez Smith, *The Building of Castle Howard* (London, 1990) and K. Downes, *Sir John Vanbrugh, a Biography* (London, 1987). The last includes an important appendix which clarifies the building of the Bow Window Room at Castle Howard and argues that the year of Hawksmoor's birth may have been 1662.

H. S. Goodhart-Rendel, *Hawksmoor* (London, 1924), has some historic photographs by F. R. Yerbury. Hawksmoor's sale catalogue was published in D. Watkin, *Sale Catalogues of Libraries of Eminent Persons*, IV (London, 1972).

The following publications have not been noted elsewhere. R. Hewlings, 'Ripon's Forum Populi' (*Architectural History*, XXIV, 1981, pp.39–52). K. Downes, 'Hawksmoor's House at Easton Neston' (*ibid.*, XXX, 1987, pp.50–76). P. du Prey,

'Hawksmoor's "Basilica after the Primitive Christian": Architecture and Theology' (*Journal of the Society of Architectural Historians*, XLVIII, 1989, pp.38–52). G. Worsley, 'Nicholas Hawksmoor: a Pioneer Neo-Palladian?' (*Architectural History*, XXXIII, 1990, pp.60–74). R. Hewlings, 'Hawksmoor's Brave Designs for the Police' (in J. Bold and E. Chaney, (eds.), *English Architecture Public and Private*, London, 1993, pp.215–29). A group of drawings for the repair and completion of Westminster Abbey was discovered in 1993 and acquired for the Abbey Library (National Art Collections Fund, *Review*, 1994).

Acknowledgements

The Author and Publishers wish to thank the following owners for permission to reproduce photographs and drawings in their possession: The Warden and Fellows and the Librarian of All Souls: 1, 12, 13, 15, 16, 133. Royal Institute of British Architects: 3, 81, 82. Staffordshire County Record Office: 10. Trustees of Sir John Soane's Museum: 14. The Archbishop of Canterbury and the Trustees of Lambeth Palace Library: 87. The Lady Hesketh: 18. Victoria and Albert Museum: 32, 138. Lambeth Public Libraries (Surrey Collections): 47. Private Collection, Chicago: 146. The Provost and Fellows of Worcester College, Oxford: 54, 60–3, 65, 66, 72, 84, 139–41. The Provost and Fellows of the Queen's College, Oxford: 56–9. The Provost and Fellows of King's College, Cambridge: 69, 71. The Dean and Chapter of St Paul's: 74. The Trustees of the British Museum: 75, 102, 103, 107, 108, 117, 123, 134, 171, 175–6. Trustees of the Ashmolean Museum, Oxford: 79, 114–15. Bodleian Library: 70, 77, 78, 168. The Principal and Fellows of Brasenose College, Oxford: 76.

PHOTOGRAPHIC SOURCES: National Monuments Record: 11, 22, 91, 128, 131, 179, 181, 182. Warburg Institute: 135, 136. Guildhall Library: 118. Greater London Council: 170. Country Life: 156, 180. Courtauld Institute of Art: 3, 32, 69, 71, 102–3, 107–8, 123, 134, 158, 171, 175–6. Martin Hürlimann: 4. Edwin Smith: 2. A. F. Kersting: 9, 98, 124, 130, 159. Gordon Moore: 149. Sydney W. Newbery: 97. Ministry of Public Building and Works: 17. All the other photographs are the author's.

Index

Numbers in *italics* are those of illustrations. The List of Works is not indexed.